THE BATTLE WITHIN

A Soldier's Story

D1435184

Neil Spencer

THE BATTLE WITHIN

About the author

Neil served in the 1st Royal Welch Fusiliers between 2002 – 2006. He deployed to Canada and Iraq as a member of the Mortar platoon. He was medically discharged with an exemplary service record. He is now a qualified fitness instructor and endurance charity fundraiser. Married with two young children, he lives in Newport, South Wales.

Acknowledgements

Before I mention the people that helped me on my journey to bring this story to life, I would first like to tell you a little story behind my drive to write it.

Back in 2007 and only a few months after splitting with Maria, I found myself talking to an old lady whilst out drinking in Caerleon. Even though I was quite drunk and emotional, she listened to every word I had to say. During the thirty or so minute conversation, I told her about what had happened to me in Iraq and all the struggles I faced afterwards. She could have walked away, but she didn't. She just listened. Before she left she said, "Neil, you need to write a book about this". I just laughed and said "Everyone has a story to tell, no one will be interested in mine", her final words were:

"Neil, please write the book".

Over the years I quite often thought about what the lady said to me that night, but the problem was that I didn't know where to start. All of my memories were in my head. It wasn't until 2013, when during a quiet evening at home my phone beeped. Some picture messages came through sent from one of my military friends, Mike England. The pictures were from the day of the suicide bombing. I was shocked at first; they brought many of the disturbing images straight back to life and I wasn't sure how I felt about it. However, their presence flicked on the switch in my mind. I could use these to help kick start my story. This was good, after all, a picture paints a thousand words. No more than five days later I started to put pen to paper, and this book "The Battle Within" had begun.

The first person I would like to thank would be that lady who first told me to write a book, although I never did catch her name. Secondly I would like to thank Mike England. Had he not sent me those images a few years ago then I would most likely never have started writing my story, and you wouldn't be reading the book you are holding now.

A Soldier's Story

The | Battle | Within

I wish to express my sincere gratitude to Lt General Jonathon Riley, CB DSO for his kind support, guidance and constant supervision, as well as providing much needed information to build this book and get my story out there.

Much gratitude also goes to Angelo Bellandi for all the hard work he put into building the book. Angelo put in much of his own free time to help make the book as good as it possibly could be. A big thank you also goes to creative designer Sam John, for outstanding work on the cover design, and another huge thanks to Darren at Tower Print in Caerphilly for creating an outstanding masterpiece.

I would also like to express my appreciation for the following two people; Lucia D'Onofrio and Rhys Hounsell, for the time and effort that went into editing this book. Although neither are professional editors, they worked wonders to get the story portrayed to the best of their ability and helped me to clearly convey what I would like you, the reader, to feel as you read my story. A big thank you also to Rebecca Cockeram for her time proofreading the work, all of which was done in her own spare time.

Finally, I would like to say thank you to my wife Selina. You have stuck by me through thick and thin, through all of the massive ups and downs and throughout my commitment to endurance charity events, and not least the two years I have spent working on this book. For that I will be forever grateful.

It has all been for you and my boys.
Much love,
Neil

This book is dedicated to my two wonderful boys Nico and Fabio.

For them being born, gave me a reason to live again.

Chapters

Foreword

In many ways, Neil Spencer was a typical young Royal Welch Fusilier. Born in Newport, Gwent, always interested in joining the Army and once he had made a decision to do just that, the motivation changed his life for the better. Like many young lads he had not done as well as he might have done at school and worse, he had been bullied throughout his youth. However the determination to go for a military career was a turning point. He got fit – very fit – no more bullying and no more under-achieving. He sailed through recruit and infantry training. He could not get a place in the first regiment he chose, the Paras, through no fault of his own – the waiting list was just too long – so he joined the Royal Welch Fusiliers and there found plenty of others from his home town with whom he quickly settled in. His first year with the Regiment included fire-fighting duties, a three-month trip to Canada, a parachute course and specialist training. So far, so good – and not much different from the experience of a thousand others.

A Soldier's Story

Then came another turning-point. The Regiment deployed to Iraq. Iraq was never a popular war: it brought about the biggest political demonstration in the history of our country; however popular support at home rallied behind the soldiers, if not behind the intervention. Initial Iraqi enthusiasm for liberation, however, soon turned into a series of insurgencies by former Ba'athists who had lost their status, by Iranian-backed Shi'ites and by Sunni extremists backed by Al-Qua'eda. These people attacked our soldiers by indirect means, chiefly roadside bombs – I.E.D.s – and suicide missions. It was one of the latter, a two-stage attack, that caused serious injury to Neil.

The initial treatment in theatre, followed by his evacuation and follow-up surgery at home appears to have been dealt with speedily. He had the advantage of innovations in battlefield first aid that have saved lives which only ten years or so ago could well have been lost; and of the rapid reforms in hospital treatment for soldiers which came out of the scandalous mistreatment of wounded men and women early on in the Iraq war in NHS hospitals which simply were not geared up to deal with them in the way that our military hospitals were before they were closed down by Government. This is some good news, especially to me as I was then both Colonel of The Royal Welch Fusiliers and Commanding General in Iraq.

It was from here on, however, that Neil's difficulties accelerated. The story makes very uncomfortable reading for those charged with the care of our soldiers: he was, as he puts it himself, lost in the system and as a result received neither the timely physical treatment, nor the mental aftercare that he needed. The latter is less obvious but often goes deeper and it is the injury that no-one really wants to address: Governments of both colours seem happy to leave the matter largely in the hands of charities.

Why did this happen? Neil himself is not sure. I think that much has to do with the destruction of our traditional family Regiments, which was being perpetrated at that time. During that process, his Regimental family, who would under the old circumstances have kept a tight grip on him, lost him. The loss of our military hospitals must also surely be a part of this problem – no matter how good Selly Oak was at reconstructive surgery, or Headley Court and Tedworth House were and are at rehabilitation.

Happily, Neil has recovered and although, very sadly, his injuries were such that he had to leave the service, he has a decent life and a loving wife and family. Uncomfortable reading I said, but not whingeing. This book is not a whine, it is a wake-up call. Neil is a tough man, he never backed away from danger or problems but took them head on. He was damaged by his military service but I think he would say that overall, his military service made him a better person and we should avoid falling into the trap of believing that everyone who did military service is diminished by it. This is plainly not so, and Neil Spencer is a wonderful example of that truth, even though he endured more adversity than most can imagine.

Jonathon Riley
Lieutenant-General
Late The Royal Welch Fusiliers

A Soldier's Story

The | Battle | Within

Chapter 01

Early Days

Even from a young age you could say I was destined to join the army. I was always running around with my makeshift rifle made from an old piece of wood. Walkie talkies in hand with my best buddy as we climbed over walls and through people's back gardens, believing we were on some kind of military operation. When you look at my family background though, it seemed unlikely.

I was born into a working class family in Newport, South Wales. A large town about 12 miles east of the welsh capital of Cardiff. My mother Tina worked in retail sales and my father John was a self-employed car upholsterer who was part of the family's upholstery business. The business was set up by my grandfather, and my father and his two brothers made the choice to follow in his trade. The business was run from a large shop on Corporation Road which had a flat above it. My mother and father lived in the flat and it was there that I was born. We only stayed there for 11 months before we moved into a 3 bedroomed house just over half a mile away. My mother was pregnant again and before long I had a little sister who they named Elizabeth.

It was as a toddler that I had my first brush with death. I was spending the afternoon visiting my grandmother and grandfather who had now moved into the flat above the shop. In the flat there was a large, single pane window with a seated area that ran across underneath. I was being nosy and kept running back and forth to look outside through the glass. On one occasion it nearly ended in disaster when I ran up to the window and failed to stop. My little body smashed through the glass, and only the woollen jumper I was wearing and my father's quick reactions stopped me falling 20 feet onto terra firma below. By the time I was 2 years old I had already used up one of my nine lives.

My earliest childhood memory was of time spent in the upholstery shop with my dad and grandfather; I used to earn a small amount of pocket money from them for helping to pick up the rubbish. It was only bits of old cloth and foam but I was able to use the money to buy lucky bags from the shop down the road. When you're a youngster, having money of your own makes you feel really grown up.

Most of my early childhood, including my time at nursery, was pretty much like any other with lots of playtime with the other children. That was at least, until I joined junior school. I was basically a loner in and out of school, and very quiet. I'm not sure why but I just never seemed to fit in with the other kids. I felt like an outcast and was never involved in the other kids' games. I did have a few friends I would spend time with, but even then it was like I wasn't there - my opinion was never heard and I felt invisible. I was also short and skinny, one of the shortest in my year, and with a lack of friends I soon became a target for bullies. To begin with it was only one or two tormentors I had to deal with, but before long it seemed like everyone wanted to pick on me. I hadn't done anything to them but they seemed to get pleasure out of making my life a misery. It never really got physical, apart from them pushing me or trying to trip me up, it was more mental threats, stuff to keep me on my toes. "Look out after school", that sort of thing.

I was approximately 9 years old and it was already starting to affect me. At least when I go to high school things will be different, I thought.

A Soldier's Story

By the time the summer holidays started I was already beginning to worry about what lay ahead. If I was being bullied in junior school, then what the hell is going to happen in high school? It was a much bigger place and with kids from lots of other schools there I was going to get the shit kicked out of me. With the new school term starting I settled in ok during the first week, even the bullies from my old school left me alone. Maybe they got fed up of it, but who was I kidding. The bullies from my old school just teamed up with those from other schools. I could almost lip read what they were saying… him over there, the short skinny lad…he's soft as shit…he's an easy target, and we done him big time in juniors…. he has no friends…Ha-ha…a Billy no mates. Already you can see where this is going.

Word started to get around that I was a soft touch, easy prey, and before long I was running a daily gauntlet between classes. Often being kicked and slapped as I made my way down the corridor, some would even grab my school bag and slam it into the ground before throwing it through the window. They somehow always managed to make sure my packed lunch was destroyed. I was constantly on guard, never knowing when or where the next attack was coming from. I couldn't tell the teachers either as that would just make the situation worse. I couldn't tell my father because he always told me, if someone picks on you, you hit them once - just once, very hard on the nose. They will get the message. I could see his point but my problem was that I was afraid of confrontation and didn't like fighting. Either way I had to do something, and what I did ultimately affected my education.

I started to become the class clown. I thought if I made people laugh they would be less likely to pick on me. Looking back now of course, it was a stupid idea and it wouldn't have made any difference, but back then faced with the bullies every day, I didn't know what else to do. Over time my school reports started to deteriorate and all the teachers had the same thing to say about me; Neil can work hard and produce good results when he wants to, but is very easily distracted. This was absolutely true and I knew I wasn't as stupid or as thick as I came across. However, the bullies were affecting my concentration so much that to everyone including my own family, I was dumb and immature.

There was a small group of lads I hung around with but like in juniors, I was an outcast and no one wanted to listen to what I had to say. When it came to team games like football, rugby, or rounders, there was always that one name that was last to be called out. NEIL. Maybe it was the fact that I didn't like sport - I was rubbish at all of it. That is, except for one event, and that was running. Not long distance though, only up to about 200m.

Running the 100m I was a little whippet, most likely from all the practice I got legging it from the bullies.

As for a school romance, forget it. I was lucky if I got a Christmas card from a girl. A kiss or relationship was out of the question and needless to say, my confidence suffered a lot. Most of the other boys my age were going out with girls from school, but for me, I hardly got the opportunity to strike up a conversation. It was just another setback.

The bullying continued daily and leaving school at the end of the day was a nightmare. I had to catch the bus home which was risky because when the bullies saw me getting on the same bus as them, they'd make sure I was toast by the time I got home. Each day I would hide around the corner watching them line up for the bus, and only once they had boarded and gone upstairs would I run to get on the bus myself. Even after I was safely on the bus, I would sit near the door for fear that I'd need to make a run for it.

Over the 5 years in high school leaving daily with the anxiety caused by these bullies, it really took it out of me mentally. Not just in school time but weekends too. I was so anxious about going back when Monday came around that my weekends were ruined as well. By the time I came to sit my GCSE exams it was too late, I had blown any chance of getting decent grades. Once I had finished my exams my grades were as expected. Shit. I knew deep down that I was capable of much more than my grades reflected, but in the real world that didn't matter, only what the papers say, and the results say: I'm dull.

A Soldier's Story

The | Battle | Within

Did I still want to join the army? Well sort of, but my confidence had taken a battering and nobody expected me to amount to anything. I was a failure to myself and my family. When I went to the job centre, reality hit. Every job I looked at seemed to be out of my league. I'd be lucky if I ended up sweeping the roads at this rate. Naturally my only real option was a recruitment company, so I signed up with a company called Kelter Recruitment that was based in town. They didn't have any real work for me but they did offer me a place on their 6-week in-house course that would earn me an NVQ Level 1 in electronics.

The pay was a mere £45 a week and could hardly be considered a wage, but it was better than nothing. After my training I was told they would find me full time work where I could utilise my new skill.

The course was easy and covered mostly printed circuit board (PCB) assembly and soldering. As soon as the course was over, as promised, I was offered a job at a Panasonic warehouse. The job was alright and paid a reasonable wage, but it didn't last and I soon found myself unemployed. Over the next 12 months I ended up in a variety of different jobs, all of which offered little financial security or job satisfaction. I even worked as a security guard at one point, back then before the days of SIA rules, anyone could do the job even if you had a string of criminal convictions. I later started working for the budget supermarket Kwik Save. It was based 11 miles away in Pontypool, so because I couldn't drive, my father used to drop me off and in the evening I would find my own way home. One Friday evening I planned to hit the clubs after work but the bus wasn't running and I didn't have money for a taxi. To make things worse, with my shirt, trousers and shoes, I was hardly kitted out for a jog home. I turned it into a fast walk and two and half hours later I finally made it home. A further 45 minutes later and I was showered, dressed, and in town sipping a chilled pint of Guinness. That was my first taste of a long distance walk.

Another job became available at a furniture manufacturing factory in Rogerstone, and because my uncle worked there as their top designer I was given the job. It was a good place to work, I started at 08:00 and finished at 16:30. My days were spent making the fabric faces that go on the front of sofas, along with other production line stuff. I was also in the process of learning to drive and things were starting to look up.

After a few months of lessons, I passed my test and took out a loan for £1,000 to purchase my very own car. Naturally I wanted something sporty. My father used to own a Ford Escort XR3I which I loved and I really wanted one for myself. But being 18 years old and inexperienced, there was no way I could afford to insure one. I had to look for something else.

I came across a Nissan sunny coupe in black. It looked like the Knight Rider car and the owner only wanted a grand for it so I bit his hand off at the chance. As soon as I brought it home I set about trying to tart it up a bit. Chrome racing pedals, a loud exhaust tail pipe, and a Kenwood CD player just for starters.

The problem was, like most teenage lads who have just passed their test, I thought I was highly skilled behind the wheel. But unlike Stirling Moss...I was not. I became a bit of a boy racer, I was young, immature, and to be honest quite foolish. It goes without saying, I had several close encounters with other vehicles.

I was no longer this short skinny lad either; it was as if I grew up overnight. After all the years of bullying and the life of failure I was facing I decided it was time for me to fight back, time to prove my worth, to show people I'm no walk over and cannot be beaten!

I was still working at the upholstery factory at the time, but not for much longer. One day when I got home from work I told my parents that I was planning to join the army, and that I was going into the careers office in the morning for more information. "What you joining?" My dad asked. "The parachute regiment", I said. My father thought I was mad. He did have a point. I was scared of heights for a start, and as for my fitness, well, I wasn't even sure.

A Soldier's Story **The | Battle | Within**

I went out for a short run just to find out, and after less than a mile I had to turn back as I couldn't breathe. Years of heavy smoking had finally caught up with me. If I was going to prove my worth to the doubters, something had to happen.

To start off with I quit the fags, and then joined a gym. The gym was only a 5-minute walk away so it was ideal. I began training straight away but was slow to start. Fifteen minutes on the treadmill and I was knackered, but things would soon change, including my attitude. Before long I was training like a pro, there were no more 20 minute sessions. I started to train twice a day, for 2 hours at a time. In the morning I'd hit the weights, then I would do 2 hours of cardio in the evening. My routine was: 1 hour on the treadmill covering around 14km, followed by 30 minutes on the bike and 30 minutes on the rowing machine. I was becoming super fit and could run 5 miles in 30 minutes. I also began to try a bit of speed marching. I had a cheap camping backpack that I stuffed with pillows for padding, and a 15kg dumbbell to add weight. I used to walk as fast as I could from my house to the 14 Locks Canal Centre, 4 miles each way taking me around 2 hours to finish. The minute I felt fit enough, I went back to the careers office.

As I walked through the door, a recruiting sergeant approached me. "How can I help?" I replied by simply saying, "I want to join the Para's". Like most jobs, staff have targets to meet, and army recruitment is no different. They want you to join their regiment because it looks good for them and also keeps the numbers up in the regiment. They will always try their best to convince you. "How about joining a welsh infantry regiment?" "No thanks," I said, "I've made up my mind". After about 10 minutes of him showing me some video clips of the welsh regiments, he gave in. "Ok Neil, the parachute regiment. A weekend insight course at their Aldershot Barracks will give you a taste of the regiment and also a chance to see how you stand up in terms of fitness. I will book you in on the next available course and once you get there, work hard and give it your all".

I had a few weeks to wait before the course began so I made sure I sustained my fitness to stay in tip top condition. The day I arrived at Aldershot station I met up with a load of other lads from all over the country who were also joining me on the course. We were chatting about what they might have planned for us when a number of Land Rovers turned up. They were there to take us to the regiment's barracks. Once we got to the barracks we were taken to the accommodation block and issued with a bed space and some itchy brown blankets. Looking at the bed I wasn't sure if the floor was more comfortable. We were then ushered into a lecture room for a briefing with the training CSM and some of the training staff. The CSM gave us a quick introduction of himself and his staff, the weekend's itinerary, and what was required of us. Which as the Para's put it, was: plenty of grit, guts and gumption.

After the briefing we had a chance to chill out in the NAAFI and talk to some of the serving lads. One piece of advice they bestowed upon us was to stick to the "2-pint rule" as there was plenty of physical work coming up in the morning. It's fair to say that not everyone stuck to it. At 05:30 the following morning, the training staff came in to wake us up. "Right you lot, get your bed space squared away, get dressed in your PT kit and be outside in fifteen". We lined up in two ranks and walked smartly to the canteen for breakfast. We were not yet in the military so there was no marching requirement. The choice of food was awesome, you had the healthy option like fruit, cereal and toast - or like me you could go for the fry-up.

Half an hour after eating we had to get ready for our first test of the day. The Basic Fitness Test ("BFT"). The BFT consisted of three tests against the clock; press ups and sit ups with the maximum number of reps you could manage in 2 minutes, followed by a timed run over 3 miles. I can't remember what I scored on the first two tests but I know I passed. As we lined up outside for the run, the regiment's PTI came out carrying two black bags. He tipped them out and a load of old combat boots fell out. He shouted, "Right then, find a pair that fits and get lined up behind me". Rummaging through the pile I found a worn pair of size 9's and chucked them on. Looking around at the other guys I could see all shapes and sizes, some were wiry fit looking men and some looked like they could move mountains. As far as the military is concerned, size doesn't matter. Only the will to win.

A Soldier's Story **The | Battle | Within**

The PTI set the pace and we had 15 minutes to cover the first mile and half. It was easy and I barely broke a sweat, though some of the boys were already falling behind. The halfway point was at queen's parade, a large grassy area in the middle of Aldershot military town. We had a 30 second rest before the return leg. "Right," said the PTI, "this is now individual best effort and you're looking for nine and a half minutes' tops, don't be the last man home…. standby…. GO". I sprinted off but the boots slowed me down more than if I had been wearing my trusty old trainers. There were about six lads in front of me and they were flying. I had the PTI on my heels telling me to catch up to them but I couldn't, I was exhausted.

I reached the final straight and saw that the fastest runners were already home. The first man finished in less than 7 minutes, a staggering time in trainers but in boots it was even more impressive. I crossed the line breathless in 9 minutes 4 seconds, not brilliant but still well within the cut off time, and some were still coming in after 12 minutes.

After the physical tests we had a shower before being given a tour of the museum and an introduction to P Company. P company, or Pre Parachute selection course, was a number of tests that have to be passed before you are accepted onto parachute training and can serve with the airborne forces. It's known as the toughest British Army selection course outside of the Special Forces. There's a log run, stretcher carry, milling, high level confidence course, plus two, ten, and twenty-mile endurance marches to complete. The events are run over a week and if you score enough points, you pass. That evening we enjoyed some more down time in the NAAFI with only the beep test to complete in the morning.

We had a final chat with the CSM about our performance over the weekend, and the next steps from there, before we were given a packed lunch and dropped back at the station. Sadly, or more stupidly, after only a few days being back home, it all went wrong. I ended up crashing my car into a roundabout and wrote it off. My car was wedged into a barrier and no matter how hard I tried, it wouldn't move. My mate gave me a lift home to collect my tool box so I could remove the bumper and free my car. When I returned to the crash scene however, the police had turned up and eye witnesses had come forward to give statements about my driving.

I was charged with four offences. Dangerous driving, racing on a public highway, hit and run, and failing to report an accident. This was madness, apparently it was a hit and run because I hit the barrier and left the scene without leaving my details. Er ok, I thought. Failing to report the accident? I felt sure I had 24 hours to notify them and they had spoken to me at the scene of the accident only an hour later. The other two offences I couldn't argue with. With statements now taken, I was awaiting a court appearance.

When I went back to the careers office and told them what happened, they said, "Your report from Aldershot was good, but unfortunately you can't continue your application until the case is settled". No way. I was gutted but I couldn't blame anyone, it was my own stupid fault. I should at least be relieved that no one was injured or killed. I had no choice but to wait for the court outcome, but time and time again it was adjourned. This happened six times before a final verdict was eventually given. Me and my mate stood in the dock while the verdict was read out. My mate was only being done for racing and was cleared of the charge. I was cleared of all but one - dangerous driving. My punishment was a 12-month ban with an extended retest and a fine of £825.

I went back into the careers office to inform them of the outcome, and this time was told I couldn't continue until my fine had been paid off. Bloody hell, was this ever going to happen? With the wages I was earning it would take ages. I only had to pay a repayment plan of £15 a week but I needed to pay a lot more if I was ever going to get signed up. After several months of paying off the fine, my father generously paid off the last of what I owed. Maybe he was fed up of my troublemaking and wanted me out of the house too.

This time when I went back to the careers office I was feeling confident, but once again I was hit with another setback. Op Barras, the daring rescue that saw men from 1 Para and 22 SAS attack the west side boys, the brutal militia group who were holding a number of members from the Royal Irish Regiment hostage. Except for the loss of one man, the operation was a success and raised publicity for recruitment of the Para's. For me though it was bad news, as my recruiter told me I now had several months on the waiting list for the Para's, or I could go with my second choice. As part of the recruitment process you choose three different units in the event of shortage or other reasons. My first choice was obviously Para reg, my second was the Royal Welch Fusiliers ("RWF"), and my third was the military police. Now with a long wait for the Para's, I was met with the choice of joining RWF which had a shorter waiting time. It wasn't an ideal situation but I could hardly go back home without some positive news, and anyway I thought, when I pass out of training I can just request a transfer. That was the plan anyway.

Before I could begin training I still had tests to complete. One was called the British Army Recruitment Battery ("BARB"), a simple touch screen test that considers your school grades and determines what role you'd be most suitable for. It was an easy test with questions such as, "If this cog turns this way, which way does this one turn?", not exactly rocket science.

Another thing I had to pass was the recruit selection centre which was run at Pirbright and covered an assortment of tests, including a medical and some physical trials. I ended up being sent home within an hour of turning up. I failed the medical. It seems I forgot to mention that I had asthma as a child and required a doctor's note before I could continue. The second time everything went well and I passed all of the tests with flying colours. All that was left to do now was the Oath of Allegiance. I signed the oath at the careers office in front of a military officer and thought, this is it, I'm finally in the Army and have a career that could last 20 years or more. Was I happy? You bet.

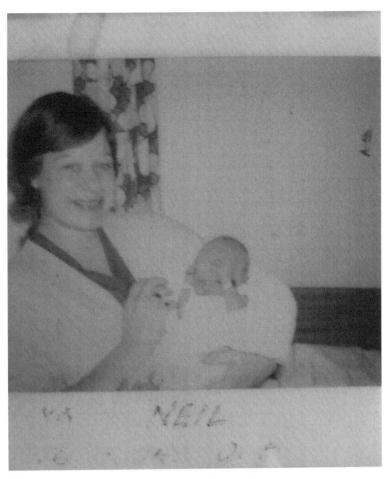

Earliest photo opportunity. With my mother just 16 hours old.

Chapter 02

A New Recruit

I couldn't wait for the 2 weeks to pass so I could begin my training. The training was going to last for 26 weeks in total, provided I didn't pick up an injury or get back-squadded. The first 12 weeks made up the first phase known as Basic Training or the common military syllabus as it's generally called, and would take place in Lichfield.

Basic training was all about taking you from your civilian life and getting you to the level of skill and discipline a trained soldier has, and ready to learn your new trade. After you complete your basic training you move on to phase 2 - trade training. It doesn't matter what role in the military you are training for; be it infantry, engineering, military police or even a chef, everyone has the same 12 weeks of basic training with only the trade training being different in length.

My trade training was to take place at the infantry training centre in Catterick, a military town stuffed away in the north Yorkshire moors. These intense 14 weeks were known as the Combat Infantryman Course and produced some of the best and most inspired infantrymen the world over. These days soldiers complete both their phase 1 and 2 at Catterick, but back in 2002, phase 1 was held in Lichfield.

The day arrived for my training to begin, and I boarded the train from Newport to Lichfield with my suitcase packed full of new clothes and a kit list of items I needed to take with me. Of course, Kiwi black shoe polish was a must. As the train pulled into Lichfield station I could see that the place was full of lads from all over the country, ready to begin a new journey of life.

A coach soon turned up with a few members of training staff. A corporal shouted out,

"One straight line facing me. When I call your name out, you reply with 'Yes Corporal'. Ok. From the Left. Smith?"
"Yes corporal."
"Roberts...? Roberts...? Roberts...!"
"Yes corporal."
"Wake up Roberts, get down and give me 20 press ups. Count them out."
"Spencer?"
"Yes corporal."

Apart from one person everyone was accounted for.

"Right, get your luggage in and get yourselves on the coach."

This was it, no going back now. The shock of capture.

Once we arrived at Whittington Barracks we were escorted to our rooms and given an hour to settle into our new environment. Including myself, there were eight of us in the room. We were complete strangers at that moment, but you could be sure that by the end of our training we would know each other better than we knew ourselves or our own families. We were chatting amongst ourselves when a member of the training staff came into the room.

A Soldier's Story **The | Battle | Within**

"Alright lads, my name is Corporal Mann and I will be your training instructor for the duration of your time here at Lichfield. When you speak to me you will address me as 'Corporal'. I'm here to make sure you get through this course so if you have any problems please don't be afraid to ask."

The initial week was going to be pretty straightforward with a bit of paperwork to fill out and another medical exam to go through. With the administration out of the way it was time for us to visit the stores and issued with our new kit, and there was a lot of it.

2 pairs of socks
2 pairs of trousers
2 shirts
2 jackets
1 Gore-Tex jacket and matching trousers
2 pairs of boots
A helmet
One S10 respirator
And all of our gym kit which consisted of a pair of shorts, a t-shirt, and a fancy pair of trainers called Silver Shadows, all crammed into a large black holdall.

It weighed us down as we struggled to carry our stuff back to our rooms. This lot of gear was only part of the kit as we would be collecting our load-carrying equipment after lunch. We lined up in circle as the quartermaster passed out more kit.

120 litre Bergen
Webbing pouches and straps
Mess tins
A digging tool
A large sleeping bag with Gore-Tex liner
Plus, a single foam roll mat

We were sent back to our rooms and found a laminated piece of A4 paper on our beds, revealing a detailed locker arrangement. By the following morning we were all expected to have our kit set out exactly as it was shown on the layout. Later that day Corporal Mann came to teach us some skills. Sadly, it wasn't shooting skills we would be learning that day but those of another deadly weapon...the steam iron.

He spent 2 hours demonstrating how we were expected to iron each piece of clothing, with only intentional creases permitted. The creases of sleeves and the front pleats of trousers had to be so sharp they looked like they could draw blood. These creases were the result of high heat, plenty of steam and a spray of starch, combined with some good old elbow grease. After Corporal Mann had finished showing us what to do, we then had to spend all evening going over every single one of our items to prepare for the locker procedure.

He showed us how to fold t-shirts using a piece of A4 paper as a guide and how to fold socks correctly. The socks were a good one as they displayed a face when packed in the locker. For the first 4 weeks they had a sad face, for 4 - 8 weeks it was a regular face, and for the closing 4 weeks, as you can probably guess, a happy face.

Most of us were up well past midnight, making sure we had completed the task properly and everything looked immaculate. After only a few hours' sleep it was time to get up and get ready for the 05:30 locker inspection. We were dressed smartly in our well pressed, brand new military uniforms, when we heard the order, "Stand by your beds!"

As the training corporal approached the bed we had to slam our left foot down into the floor whilst shouting out our name, rank and number. The training corporal would then start inspecting our bed space like a crime scene investigator. No matter how much time and effort was put in, you could be sure that the training staff would find something that wasn't quite up to standard.

Later on in the day came what I was dreading the most. The Haircut. I was quite young looking anyway and struggled to buy fags without ID so I knew

A Soldier's Story

it was going to be dramatic. I sat apprehensively in the chair as the clipper was set to number 1 and buzzed all over my scalp. The after effect was a right piss take. I looked about 12 years old and ready to join the cadets, not the big boys Army. Along with my freshly shaved head and new uniform, I looked like I had just stepped out of a catalogue.

I was starting to make some good friends during training and had become close to a couple of guys, Dave Harris and Lagi-Lagi. Dave was joining the Fusiliers like me and was motorbike mad. Lagi was a mountain of a man standing at about 6ft 4 and 18 stone of muscle. Lagi was not the sort of person you'd want to upset. He came from Fiji and was one of the quietest people I'd ever met. I guess being a man of his size he'd learned the art of self-control, otherwise he could do some real harm if he wanted to. Only once did I ever see him lose his temper when some idiot was spoiling for a fight. Picking on Lagi was not the brightest idea this lad had come up with and it took a large number of men to restrain Lagi and stop him from tearing the antagonising little shit apart.

During the next few weeks we were taught the basics of marching with hours spent going up and down the parade square until our ankles were burning. For some of the boys it took a little time to get used to it as they lacked the prerequisite co-ordination. This was evident in the way they would move both left arm and left leg at the same time, also known as "tick tocking".

We also whiled away the hours in the classroom learning about military history, the military rank structure, map reading and basic first aid.

In our second week we were introduced to our personal weapon: the SA80 assault rifle. There was a lot of class work to cover before we would get the chance to unleash on the firing range though. It was, in fact, week 5 before we would even visit the range. During lessons we were taught the working principles of the weapon, how to fully strip, assemble and clean the weapon, before moving on to the handling drills of how to load and unload safely, as well as how to deal with stoppages and other troubleshooting advice. Weapon safety was paramount, and only once the instructors believed we had acquired the necessary skill and respect owed to the weapon would we be allowed to use live rounds on the range.

Towards the end of week 2 we got our first taste of living in the field during "Exercise First Night" where you spend two nights out in the field. Living in the field is an important aspect of training and one that can take a lot of people by surprise. We had to learn how to pack a Bergen properly which is a skill in itself. As a kid on a fishing trip for example you would most likely throw all of your kit into a rucksack in any old order and it would suffice. But that's not how things work in the military. A Bergen contains the complete kit required to survive while out on the ground. It's like carrying a house around on your back, and like your house, it should be clean and serviceable with everything in its place.

A fully packed Bergen can weigh upwards of 100lbs, so it needs to be prepared correctly and in good order. Ideally, things like spare clothes, your sleeping bag, things you might only use now and again, all go at the bottom of the bag, with the things you need most towards the top. Items like Gore-Tex and warm kit can go in the top flap or side pouches for quick access, along with your food and water.

While out in the field we learned how to build a shelter and how to patrol at night using only hand signals. It was all really exciting stuff, apart from night sentry. Being woken up at 02:00 to sit in what could be a water filled ditch for 2 hours was not the most pleasant of experiences but it was all an essential part of military life that everyone had to experience.

Week 5 approached and it was almost time for us to visit the live firing range, but first we had to pass the weapon handling test. One by one we were called into a room where an instructor would throw a load of commands at us, all of which had to be demonstrated without fault. Everything was covered in the test from loading to unloading, to making safe and stoppage drills. Some people needed a second chance but everyone got there in the end with only one person having difficulty passing. Lagi.

That evening I managed to get hold of a rifle replica made from a piece of wood, and after spending 2 hours with Lagi going over and over all the exercises, he passed the test with flying colours the next day.

A Soldier's Story

The | Battle | Within

After Lagi passed his test we went out onto the range and practised our shooting to distances of 400m, using a range of different firing positions. Once the weapons were zeroed, hitting targets out to 100m was little more than point and shoot, but beyond that range the fall of the round and the wind direction had to be taken into consideration and adjusted accordingly.

Soon enough week 6 was upon us and we were already halfway through phase 1. We had a marching test to pass first, and a few questions on the history of the regiment you were joining. If we passed both of them then we'd earn a long weekend at home. Even better, upon our return we could replace our baseball caps for regimental berets. In my historical test I was asked when the Royal Welch Fusiliers were formed.

"1689 sir."
"Correct."

That was it, I had gotten myself a weekend in my own bed! Everyone was pleased. We had only known each other for 6 weeks but we were living in each other's' pockets 24/7 and had become a brotherhood. It would be a shame to see someone have to stay the weekend when most people were back home. Everyone deserved the break.

When I arrived at Newport station I was surprised to see my father waiting there for me. It wasn't like him so I knew something was wrong. He didn't have good news.

"While you've been away your mother was diagnosed with breast cancer. She's waiting for a date to begin treatment"

Bloody hell, what could I say? I didn't have a clue, I thought I would play it by ear. When I saw her I thought the best thing to do was to be positive, but instead she was the more positive one by acting totally normal and asking how my training was going. I tried not to mention the cancer and just told her how I was getting along.

Most of the weekend was spent in the pub with nights out in a club or two, just making the most of my freedom. The weekend flew by and it was soon time to return to Catterick. I gave my mother a kiss and wished her well as she was soon going to be starting chemotherapy.

The next 6 weeks were more or less the same as before but with more time spent in the field, getting rounds in at the range and just generally getting on with our training. We also had another BFT to see how we fared after 8 weeks of gym sessions and forced speed marches. By this point I just wanted to get it over with and thought, bring on phase 2.

As soon as we picked up our No.2 parade uniform we knew we were inching closer to the passing out parade. When week 12 arrived, our final week, it turned out to be the longest week in history with loads of last-ditch preparations like full dress rehearsals and fitness and shooting tests. It was a proud moment for me as family and friends were invited to watch us pass out. My mother and father travelled up to see me and we had a well-earned 2 week break at home before the start of phase 2.

Most of that fortnight was spent getting pissed and catching up with friends, although in truth I really wanted to be back at camp to finish the training.

From what I had been told, phase 2 was much more relaxed, and it was true to a certain extent. There were still locker inspections and so on, but as we had passed phase 1 we were now classed as trained soldiers and were therefore expected to maintain a sense of discipline without the need for constant checks.

Phase 2 was run from Vimy barracks and as we entered the camp we were greeted by a huge sign bearing a shield and bayonet with the words, "School of Infantry", written underneath. This is where it gets real. Although this stage was going to be much more physically demanding than the first, there were some benefits. Those benefits came in the form of luxury items.

To most people they sound like trivial, insignificant things, but to us it was positively indulgent compared to what we were used to. We were allowed to use our own bedding, and could have things like TV's and PlayStations, but put one foot wrong and you would soon be back to itchy blankets and whatever music you had on your phone.

The training staff came to welcome us and I was placed under section commander Corporal Gareth Redfern. He was also a member of the Fusiliers and had gone to the same school as me although he was a few years older. He joined the Fusiliers straight from school and had a good number of years' service behind him. No doubt he had the skills and knowledge to kick us into shape. Our platoon sergeant was John Williams who was also a member of the Fusiliers.

One of the first things we had a go at was the Infantry Combat Fitness Test ("CFT"). The CFT was an 8-mile speed march through mixed terrain whilst carrying 44lbs of kit and a rifle. That's a total of 55lb to lug across 8 miles with a time limit of just 2 hours to do it in. I loved speed marching and found that I had a natural flair to walk fast as hell under a crushing load. I'm sure all the training I did alone while preparing for the Parachute Regiment was what helped build up my physical and mental endurance.

In addition to the CFT we had a multitude of other physical tests to get through, such as the Beep Test and ever present BFT.

Two weeks into training we had the bayonet drill to face, and what a day that was. From first thing in the morning we were run ragged and constantly made to feel stressed out. It was aimed at gradually building up our aggression so that when it was time to face the dummies we would go all out like men possessed. It was a long day but I fully enjoyed it, though I can't say I would feel the same doing it in a real situation.

The daily locker inspections continued, albeit at a much more laid back pace. A favourite punishment they liked to dish out was a dress parade. You were given a number of minutes to get changed into whichever kit the training staff chose to call out. This could mean going through every item in your wardrobe which you had just spent the entire evening ironing to precision.

A popular and quite a funny one was the turtle. Wearing black combat boots, green long johns and t-shirt, you would tuck your green sleeping bag into your waist, under your legs and over your back. With the helmet on you can just picture the scene.

We were allowed most weekends off but as it was too far to travel back to South Wales every weekend, some of the lads and I made use of the bars in town. There was one main hot spot we liked to frequent which was a club that just so happened to be the place every other person went too, and for good reason. Pay a small entry fee and all drinks were free. For a young squaddie this was great, but also a recipe for disaster.

One Saturday evening our night almost ended before it had even begun. It was a couple of miles walk into town and wasn't uncommon for one of us to need a piss along the way. Sprawling woodland lined our left as we walked down the road, so normally we would step over the dividing wall which was only about a foot high, walk in a few feet and do our business. On this particular evening one of the lads, a short lad whose name I can never remember, said he needed a piss. He ran ahead of us and hopped over the low wall. After a few minutes he still hadn't returned, even as we started shouting out for him, there was no reply. What the hell is he playing at? A bit puzzled, I went to take a look.

The area in which he had jumped over was in fact a bridge with a 20ft drop into a stream. He was lying there motionless, face down in the dark water. We called out to him but got no reply, and he still didn't move. Shehata, myself and an Egyptian lad climbed down to get to him. We attempted to wake him again but still no joy. We knew we had to get him back up somehow, so decided we would lift from the bottom while others at the top would pull him up towards them. Looking down from the top it was an incredibly steep and slippery bank, and although he only weighed about 10 stone, trying to lift an unconscious man proved no easy task. While we were hauling him up, another lad was on the road trying to flag down a vehicle whilst he called for an ambulance on his phone.

A Soldier's Story

We managed to get him up and thankfully he came around. The knock on the head must have been a good one to take him out for so long. We propped him up against the wall and draped a jacket over his body to keep him warm while we waited for the military police to turn up. The police took a few statements and left it at that because fortunately it was just an accident. The lad made a full recovery and was back in training the next day. Sadly, I found out years later that he had died in a motorcycle accident back home.

Another incident we had following a night out involved a group of Fijian lads. They were barely 5ft tall, but stocky as hell and strong as an ox. They were good guys and good soldiers, but they seemed to struggle with drink. After a meagre 2 pints they wanted to fight the world and became an easy target for drunken louts looking for trouble. During these alcohol-fuelled brawls, having Shehata with us was a blessing. Built like a heavyweight boxer with a punch to match, I'd never seen a man take out so many so fast. It was like a scene from the film Hooper. One evening after getting back from the club, I was woken up to find one of the Fijian lads at the foot of my bed.

"Were you in the club tonight?" he asked.
"Yeah, why?"
Crack. The punch hit me right in the chops.
"I will ask you again…. were you in the club tonight?"
"Yes…"

I'm whacked in the face again. I could feel the blood now, dripping from my nose. The punches didn't hurt, probably because I was still drunk. He ordered me to wait there while he got more of his mates to batter me. Like fuck, I thought. As soon as he left the room I got dressed and legged it round to Shehata's room.

Banging like hell on his door, as soon as he saw my face he flipped, pulling out his entrenching tool he began to screw it together.

"Bloody hell mate," I said, "it's not that serious, I don't want you to kill the bastard."

Thankfully he put it away, the last thing you need at the start of your military career is an assault charge on your record. A report was logged about what happened and we never had any more problems after that.

By this time our training had intensified and the field exercises were getting longer and longer. There was an abundance of speed marches, gym sessions crammed between time spent on the firing range, and exercises to practise our contact and patrolling skills. It was all slowly coming together and I felt at home doing something I enjoyed and was good at. Our departing exercise was a big-un: a 2-week battle camp running through everything we had been taught throughout the phases, ending with a live firing contact scenario.

The exercise was conducted in Otterburn, close to the Scottish border. The place was bloody freezing the whole time and we couldn't wait to just be done with it all. It was an exhausting and challenging experience but thoroughly enjoyed all round. With the final exercise completed, we were now free to relax a little and look forward to our passing out parade.

The final passing out parade was a cracking day, my parents came up from Newport to see me and once the presentations were over we all headed for the NAAFI for a few pints. I now had 2 weeks of leave to look forward to before joining my regiment at Aldershot.

Chapter 03

Military Life

I spent most of the 2 weeks back home in pubs and clubs. Although I was still in the early days of my military career, I felt a great sense of personal pride and achievement, and with the prospect of a possible 22 years to serve, I was going to make the most of it. Joining my regiment couldn't come round quick enough.

The regiment was based at Normandy Barracks in Aldershot having just moved from Turnhill. I collected my rail warrant and loaded up with my new kit, leaving Newport train station ready for the start of my new life. Once I got to Aldershot I took a taxi to the barracks. I couldn't bloody believe it when John Saunders, a lad I knew from school, came out of the guard room to greet me.

"Didn't know you were bloody coming!" he said, obviously surprised to see me, although later on he informed me that there were quite a few lads from Newport on camp. He took me into the guard room while I waited to find out where I was supposed to be going.

Halfway through a cup of coffee, a platoon sergeant arrived and gave me a brief welcome to the Fusiliers before instructing me to grab my kit and get moving. He led me to the accommodation block saying, "Ok Spence, you're going into 4 platoon, B Company. Drop your kit here and sort your stuff out. The rest of the company are out on a speed march but they won't be long."

While sorting through my stuff the rest of the platoon came bursting through the door, dripping in sweat. Another lad I recognised from my school years, Daniel Edwards, was also in B Company. How many more bloody people was I going to bump into down here? I soon found out that it was quite a few.

I settled into my new home right away, and with the recruit training out of the way, it was more or less like a 9 to 5 job. Unless you were on operations, exercise, or guard duty, you could go home on weekends and there was far less bullshit.

I'd been in the regiment for a couple of weeks when one day I was making my way into B Company Headquarters and saw something interesting on the notice board. It was a poster inviting people to sign up to the parachute course. This, I thought, was my chance to prove myself to those who had said I'd never make it as a Para because I was scared of heights.

I swiftly added my name to the list.

A couple of weeks later, 4 platoon were being punished on the parade ground because a cigarette butt had been found under a bed during inspection. I was in the middle of being run ragged when a runner appeared to tell me that the Sergeant Major wanted to see me in his office. I walked to his office wondering what the hell I could have done.

"Sir, you wanted to see me?" I said as I stood across his desk.
"Yes Spence, you and Aled Morgan have been picked for the parachute course this Monday. You still up for it?"
"Yes, sir!"
"Good" he replied.

A Soldier's Story   **The | Battle | Within**

I was quickly excused from the rest of the hammering my colleagues were enduring, and told to get my shit together, ready to report to Netheravon Camp at 09:00 the following Monday. And that was that. I could now look forward to 2 weeks' worth of jumping out of aeroplanes. I was thrilled.

Aled and I rocked up nice and early Monday morning to begin the course. It was run by the Joint Service Parachute Centre ("JSPC") and virtually every instructor there had completed a minimum of 1000 jumps with some even reaching 5000. There was a bunch of us on the course with the majority of lads being Royal Marines.

The type of parachute we used was a ram-air design which was rectangular in shape to make it extremely agile. We were doing static line jumping which in simple terms means that the parachute deploys automatically once you jump out of the aircraft. Our canopy container was attached by a long webbing strap which was secured to the aircraft at the other end. After you jump, the strap reaches its maximum length and becomes taut, opening the container to release the main chute.

We had at least 6 hours of ground training to cover before we would get the chance to jump as there was a lot to go over; leaving the aircraft safely, what to do in the event of malfunction, the usual safety advice. Most importantly, in the event of an emergency, we were shown how to use the Parachute Landing Fall ("PLF") which is a technique used the world over to minimise risk of injury.

The basics are that you keep your legs together and slightly bent, elbows tucked in, and as soon as you touch the ground you slightly twist your body so you fall into a roll. In theory the kinetic energy will pass through your whole body rather than just your legs.

On the front of the harness were two safety toggles, one to cut away your main chute and the other to deploy the reserve.

We also carried a Cypress which is a brand of Automatic Activation Device ("AAD"). In the event of malfunction or injury, the job of the AAD is to deploy the reserve chute.

The AAD was pre-set to a height of 1000ft and would deploy the chute should we drop below that range uncontrollably.

Once the instructors were happy with our drills on the ground, it was time for the real thing.

We jumped from between 3500ft and 5000ft out of a Cessna, and it was a good 15-minute ride to get up to jump height. Once the jump-master had checked that we were over the drop zone, he called us over one at a time to the door. I vividly recall watching each person nervously inching forward on their knees, and counting down until it was my turn.

I got myself into position and hovered at the edge, looking down. Even though we'd been told it wasn't a good idea, I couldn't resist. Bloody hell I wish I had listened.

I plunged through the opening and started going through my drills. One thousand.... two thousand.... three thousand.... four thousand.... check canopy. I looked up and everything was going smoothly. I grabbed the steering toggles and tested them.... left turn.... right turn.... all good.

Now I was happy, I had to locate the drop zone and aim for it. The canopy had a natural forward speed of 20mph, so if you had a 20mph wind behind you it would mean an overall speed of 40mph. I had an altimeter on my wrist which showed me my height and was used to help you land. You land similar to an aircraft by flying into the wind. At 1000ft you head downwind, at 500ft you head cross wind and at 300ft you turn into the wind. This is known as "holding" and helps to slow down the canopy.

As the ground drew nearer, I checked the altimeter. 100ft.... 80ft... 60ft... 40ft... 20ft... 10ft … and flare. I pulled both toggles down firmly, putting the brakes on for a nice two footed landing. With my first solo jump completed, I felt amazing. Although I was bloody terrified of heights, I had overcome my fear and trusted my life to a bit of cord and nylon. Back in the hangar we watched a video of our jumps to examine any errors and help us perfect our form. I managed a good first jump. My head stayed up and I demonstrated a good, stable exit followed by good canopy control and landing.

A Soldier's Story **The | Battle | Within**

Aled was doing fine as well and over the next couple of jumps I progressed to dummy pulls. Dummy pulls are also static line jumps but while falling you must simulate pulling a ripcord, usually an old rolled up newspaper. After three successful dummy pulls you could then move on to free-fall.

Unfortunately, I didn't get a chance to try free-fall jumps as the wind picked up and put a stop to all jumps for the rest of the course. During the 2 weeks we only managed to fit in four jumps. It would be in Canada the following year before I would get another chance.

Back in Aldershot, the regiment along with many others, were getting ready for a different type of operation. Operation Fresco. The Fire Brigades Union ("FBU") were planning strike action to secure a better salary. The FBU demanded a 39% pay rise which would increase the average firefighter's salary to around £30,000. All three branches of the Armed Forces had the task of providing emergency cover if it went ahead. A training plan was put together.

We would have several weeks of training ahead to get up to speed on the equipment and vintage Green Goddesses would be our fire-fighting weapon. The Goddesses dated back to the 1950's and were very basic with no radios, cutting equipment or power steering. On top of that, with a cruising speed of only 45mph it could take some time to get to a call out. They could do the job though, and after all, the British military is the best in the world for getting on with whatever they're given.

We learned about ladder drills, how to connect and hold the hoses safely and how to use fire hydrants and the external water pump. As for going into buildings, that was a no-go. There wasn't the time or the resources to train us for that. All of the indoor work was left to members of the Royal Navy and Royal Air Force. They provided Breathing Apparatus Rescue Teams ("BART") and Rescue Equipment Support Teams ("REST"). Our team worked well together and we felt ready, if necessary, to hit the streets. To be honest it would've been better for all concerned if the FBU didn't strike, although that didn't stop me secretly hoping they did. It was something different and we trained for it, we just needed the go ahead. It was eventually confirmed, the first strike would be Wednesday 13th November.

We loaded up the Green Goddesses and headed for our Area of Operations ("AOO"). My regiment was assigned to cover central London. Each company was assigned a temporary fire station from locations spread throughout the city. My team would be working from Chelsea Barracks. We split into groups; two day teams and two night teams.

The Metropolitan Traffic Police were based with us for the duration of the strike, to provide us with an escort. They would be essential. We weren't familiar with the area and if an emergency came through we had to get there as soon as possible, there would be no time for maps or a sat nav. We also had a high ranking fire officer on standby to provide professional advice if needed.

While we were stood down we made use of the beautiful scenery around Chelsea. Early morning runs around Chelsea Embankment and through Hyde Park were a lot less boring than the usual circuit around Aldershot. I took advantage of our surroundings and did a spot of sparring in the gym as I had recently joined the company boxing team.

The day of the strike arrived and it was planned to last 48 hours beginning at 18:00. This was what I'd secretly been hoping for. This was my shift. At 18:00 we were eagerly standing by in our Gore-Tex, readily waiting for the first call. Twenty minutes into the shift, our first call came through. An accommodation block was on fire a few miles away, but when we arrived it wasn't what we were expecting. It was a nursing block and evidently some of the trainee nurses thought it'd be funny to set a small bin alight - just to get the Army out. As funny as it might sound, it was a total waste of resources which were already pushed to the limit as it was.

We dealt with way more calls than normal, most of them deliberate and aimed at pissing us off and wasting our time. One that wasn't a prank however, was an apartment block that was ablaze. There were about five floors and the fire was on the ground floor. Me and a teammate ran into the block and up the stairs to start evacuating the building, banging hard on the doors as we made our way to the top. There was no response. As we headed back down the stairs, we realised the fumes had rapidly penetrated the building and we were suddenly overcome by smoke. I understand now how easily smoke

A Soldier's Story

can kill and can honestly say that it was a frightening experience. I pulled my jacket up over my mouth and nose, but the smoke still managed to get in. My eyes were burning and visibility had disappeared to nothing. I held my back against the wall as I tried to make my way down the staircase. I was only on the second floor and couldn't see shit. It was such a relief when I felt someone grab me and pull me out. It was a member of the BART team. It was a close call, but my own stupid fault for going into the block when we'd be instructed not to. Needless to say, I kept out of buildings after that.

With the firefighter strikes done and dusted, we had a busy period ahead of us back at Aldershot. I was moving out of B Company and into the Support Company's Mortar Platoon, whilst the whole regiment was getting ready to move into a brand new, state of the art barracks a short distance away.

Over the next few months we settled into our new digs. We now had single man rooms complete with en-suite facilities. I loved it, you had more privacy and in the evenings you could do as you pleased without worrying about anyone else.

Most evenings the lads would hang out in the other boys' rooms on the games consoles, or just messing about. I had my TV and PlayStation but most evenings I was out tabbing alone in the Aldershot training area. I loved the fitness and felt I had a natural ability for tabbing.

During my time at Mons Barracks I had the mortar qualification course to undertake as well as the Regular Radio User ("RRU") cadre. It was really fast paced and exciting. I still didn't drive as I hadn't got round to re-taking my driving test. Thankfully, there were a few lads who lived in South Wales so getting home on the weekends was no problem.

It wasn't long before we had a big exercise to look forward to with 3 months in Canada, beginning in August.

We were going to the British Army Training Unit Suffield ("BATUS"), located in Alberta. I loved the place, it was also the only place I've been to where you could drive for 4 hours and not see a bend in the road. The place was enormous. For our first 6 weeks we stayed in a Canadian forces base at Wainwright. It was incredible, a real John Wayne sort of town.

We stayed in wooden huts and ventured out in the field during the day to practice some drills, before going back to camp at around 17:00 to have the evening to ourselves. One of the high points of my time in Canada, aside from the training, was the rest and recuperation ("R&R"). We had the best part of a week in the city of Edmonton so, first thing Monday morning, we piled into the coach and headed for the city. Our only detail was to be back at the same point at noon on Friday, have fun, and stay out of trouble.

For perhaps the first time in my life I was totally happy. My mother was in remission back home, I was in a career of my choice - one I was immensely proud of - and I'd already tried out parachuting and firefighting training. Now I was living it up with 3 months in Canada. Life couldn't have been better and when I got back to the UK I had the team medic course and a 6-month tour in Iraq to look forward to.

After being dropped off in Edmonton on the Monday, there was one incident which has stuck in my mind. We were close to a McDonalds near the drop off point so a few of the lads headed over for a bite to eat before finding a hotel to stay in. After we finished eating we made our way to the Holiday Inn down the road. We put four lads to a room to save money, and save we did. It worked out at roughly £50 each for the week which was a bloody bargain if you ask me.

Two of the boys were picked to get the booze in as we wanted to have a few drinks in the room before heading to the city's nightspots later on. By 22:00 we were all pissed on Jack Daniels and ready to hit the bars. On the way out, John and I decided to have another McDonalds and being the competitive type he took off, hollering that it was a race. Unfortunately for John I ran like lightning and overtook him quickly. As I neared the entrance I failed to notice the large perspex windbreak around the seating area, and because I was drunk I was looking through it, rather than at it. I smashed face first into the

A Soldier's Story **The | Battle | Within**

barrier and the force was strong enough that I took John to the ground with me as I ricocheted off it. The outline of my face was still firmly imprinted on the perspex when we returned to McDonalds on Friday.

Another great memory of Canada was the visit to West Edmonton Mall. At the time it was the world's largest shopping mall and it really has to be seen to be believed. With over 800 stores, a full sized ice rink, water park and pirate ship, complete with seal shows, this was no normal shopping centre. Tucked away at the far side of the centre stood the Wild West shooting gallery. Bloody hell, a real life shooting range in a shopping centre. For around £30 you could take hold of a whole variety of different 9mm hand guns and unleash 50 rounds down the range. An unbelievable sight when compared to the UK.

With the R&R over it was time to get back to training with a tough exercise at BATUS.

Thousands of troops and vehicles screaming over the Canadian prairie in a very realistic battle group scenario, with lasers on our weapons and vehicles, it was like a gigantic game of laser quest.

It was a rough old exercise and it was also the most time I had spent in the field in one outing - 3 weeks. Three long weeks without a decent night's sleep, tasty hot meal or a proper wash. It really makes you appreciate the small things in life when you return home.

The weather was unlike anything I'd seen before either. When we arrived in August it was the same as a good British summer, with temperatures up in the 70's. By the time we came to leave in November, it had dropped to -10, or -20 with the wind chill, and there was about 2ft of snow.

Almost too soon, it was time to leave this incredible country and head home. When we got back we had a week off and a chance to catch up with family and friends. Regimental life was fairly quiet until after Christmas and then the diary was once again full of commitments. There was a hectic 8 weeks ahead because in April we were heading to Iraq on Operation Telic 4 for 6 months. I just had my team medic cadre to complete, which would be no problem.

I was already planning my life post-Iraq and had decided that once the tour was over I was keen to attempt the infamous Special Air Service ("SAS") selection course. The biggest disadvantage I had was that on the surface I was still a fresh recruit and considered relatively inexperienced having served just over 2 years. What I did have in my favour though was my high level of physical fitness combined with a rock solid, never quit attitude. I was using Iraq as my first taste of combat and proof that I could stand up to the test of soldiering properly in a real warzone.

Aspiring to join the regiment was not about black clad figures abseiling down embassies or being James-Bond-daring. It was more about what they represented, and that was the ultimate as far as being a soldier is concerned. In the regular Army there was no need to be motivated or self-disciplined as the platoon sergeant and sergeant majors were there to make sure that you did what was required. Special forces soldiers were more or less left to their own devices. They're highly trained and self-disciplined, and don't require senior staff checking on their every move. It was a much more mature and laid back image and one that I aspired to be a part of.

In the meantime, training for Operation Telic 4 began in earnest.

Chapter 04

Iraq

Prior to our deployment we had a briefing in the lecture hall with the Operational Training and Advisory Group ("OPTAG") on the pre-deployment training we would be undertaking. This began with a PowerPoint presentation followed by a film showing us the current situation in Southern Iraq, it was a little bit about the daily life but most importantly, the reality of the conflict and the challenges we were likely to face. The video also contained some graphic images, and to be fair the pictures were a massive wakeup call. Seeing those images of guys with gunshot wounds, missing limbs and the effects of nuclear and biological warfare, it really made you sit up in your chair and take note of what was lying in wait.

Our OPTAG training was broken down into different areas and covered all the likely situations we might encounter, as well as the Standard Operating Procedures ("SOP's") to deal with them. We broke off into little groups of around 15 men and over the period of a week we spent several hours going over the training.

The first lesson my group had was on the Arabic language and a friendly Iraqi man in his mid-40s was given the task of training us. They didn't expect us to be fluent of course, but we were expected to grasp some of the basics. Things like how to greet someone, and ask a person's name were important, and it also fed into the "hearts and minds" ethos of the deployment. If you're polite and friendly you may be able to get the locals on your side, and then half the battle is won.

The first phrase our tutor taught us was, "As-salamu alaykum", which means "peace be to you". After hearing it repeated to us a few times it was then our turn to try.

"As-salamu alaykum…As-salamu alaykum…As-salamu alaykum…", over and over we practised until it was second nature. We then moved on to the next phrase, "Wa-alakum-as salaam", which means "peace be to you also". Again we went over and over it. It was an enjoyable experience and after 2 hours I must have learned ten phrases, a lot more than I had managed after years of studying French in high school.

Further training followed with a lesson on the traditions and practises of the Muslim faith. A big no-no was never to wave or shake hands using your left hand as it's a sign of disrespect. Muslims use their left hand to wipe their arse so you get my point, right hands only. We also had to respect their beliefs, prayer times and general way of life.

After we completed the lifestyle and traditions phase, it was time to get back to the more serious aspect which was the training that would keep us alive on the ground. First up was how to conduct a body search for intelligence information or weapons, while working as a 2-man team. One man provided cover while the other worked his way around the body, always working from behind to make sure you don't end up with a broken nose from a quick knee to the face.

A Soldier's Story **The | Battle | Within**

Next it was vehicle check points ("VCP's") and how to stop, question, and fully search a vehicle including all the hiding places even the car manufacturers don't know about. There was public order training to follow in case of a large scale city riot, and finally to finish our training to the max came what was probably our biggest threat, that of the IED, the Improvised Explosive Device.

The IED can come in many forms but the three most common methods we were likely to encounter were from the ones carried on a person, a vehicle, or just disguised at the road side. They had - and still do - a deadly reputation and were probably the last thing you want to experience or come up against. We studied and practiced the drills for finding a device time and time again, and the plan was simple; depending on the size of the device, we would evacuate the area and set up a cordon as far out as required. Any device around the size of a mobile phone would require a cordon radius of at least 100m, and anything larger - up to vehicle size - would see that cordon stretch out to a considerable distance of 400m. These figures were just for built-up areas however, if it was open ground then the distance was doubled. That's 800m or 8 football pitches if you encountered a car bomb on open ground.

Once we finished our training it was time for one last exercise. We used a training area that consisted of a number of buildings in the layout of a village. For years soldiers have used training locations like this to fine tune their skills in patrolling and fighting in close quarters and built up areas, and for us it was no different. The village was presented as a typical Muslim town within Southern Iraq. Loud speakers played Muslim prayer hymns and mock characters roamed the streets playing the locals. For us it was a chance to put the skills we had learned during the week to the test, whilst in a safe but realistic training scenario.

When the training was done and dusted, we had a bit of down time and a chance to spend some time with family and friends before being deployed. I spent most of the time in the pub playing pool with John or in the clubs getting pissed. A lot of the lads took out loans to buy themselves some Gucci kit to take away with them, or expensive electronics with laptops being the most popular. What's £500 for a computer? When you're on deployment for half the year you can save a lot of money and more than make up for anything you spent now.

The Saturday before we left, my mother, father and I, headed to The Dodger for the night with a plan to meet up with John later. It might seem strange but I wasn't nervous or worried about going to Iraq. To be clear, this wasn't some act of bravado, I was genuinely excited and it was the precise reason I joined the Army. It's no different to a runner who spends months training in the early hours of the morning through wind and rain, building up to that one big race. At some point he just wants to run it for real. I felt the same, after months of military training exercises this was my time, this was my marathon.

I think back to that time now as a father myself, and the very thought of one of my children or even myself going off to a war zone fills me with dread. Maybe it's because I've seen the long and short term effects of combat close up, I'm not sure. But I've no doubt my mother and father must have been worried for me, even though they didn't show it at the time. Back then I was 23 years old, single, and had a career I was proud of and loved. I had few worries in life and was determined to make the most of it. I'm now 35 with a beautiful wife and two gorgeous little boys, and with all the responsibilities that comes with, I wouldn't have it any other way.

That evening in the pub was brilliant, plenty of drink and with a good few attempts on the karaoke, spirits were high. Just as the night was coming to an end the pub landlord came over and wished John and I a safe journey and promised to have a pint waiting for us upon our return.

Sunday night at home felt like the longest day ever. I wasn't leaving until 22:00 but every time I looked at the clock it had barely moved. My bags were already packed and waiting by the door, and I was starting to feel a bit restless and anxious. A couple of beers and a few DVD's helped to pass some of the time, and before long, John was knocking on the door. My mother and father waited up to see me off but I hated goodbyes at the best of times, I would much prefer to have snuck out quietly and avoid all the hugs and best wishes. But that wouldn't be right. Of course I was a little emotional, and dare I say it, I had a tear in my eye as I said goodbye to my parents.

A Soldier's Story

I had a couple of hours' kip in the car on the way back to Aldershot, and after the weekend I'd had, I certainly needed it. As soon as I got back to camp I jumped straight back into bed. I knew my uniform needed ironing but that could wait until morning. Most of the expensive stuff in my room like the TV and PlayStation had been put into storage until I returned, so I drifted off to sleep listening to the radio on my Nokia phone. I managed just a couple of hours sleep before I was back at it and starting to get my shit together. I was only packing a few luxury items to take: a disposable camera, my Sony CD player, some photos, and a hip flask given to me by my sister which she had gotten engraved for me. The flask had brandy in it, and even if I didn't drink it, it was comforting to know it was there.

The coaches were lined up on the parade square and had been there for the last hour. The amount of kit I was taking was going to require two trips to the coach. I had my Bergen, daysack and belt kit, as well as my body armour and my holdall containing all of my personal stuff. All our weapons had already been sorted out. We lined up in platoon order while a final kit check was done; documents, MOD90 (army ID card), dog tags and passports. I grabbed my CD player from the holdall before jumping on the coach.

We were flying from RAF Brize Norton on a Tristar and the flight was going to take approximately 8 hours with a short stop in Qatar. As soon as we landed in Qatar I could already feel the heat penetrating the skin of the aircraft, and the moment the doors opened it felt like you were walking into a sauna. It must have been in the mid-40's and within 20 minutes of being on the ground I was starting to feel dizzy and needed some fluid quickly. Mercifully there was a fridge stocked full of 2 litre bottles of water, so I grabbed a cold bottle and necked half the lot in one go. The symptoms quickly dissipated and I began to feel better just in time for our call to board the next flight. The flight into Basra was on a different aircraft, a Hercules transport aircraft. This flight was the less comfortable of the two, but was fortunately the shortest.

As we approached Basra, a call came over the tannoy telling us to close all window sliders and fasten our seat belts. Then unlike normal passenger planes, all the aircraft lights were turned out, sending us into complete darkness. The reason behind this was because if someone wanted to take a shot at us as we came in to land, having the lights on display just screams, "Here we are! Come and shoot us!". Turning out the lights minimises the risk to some degree, although there is little you can do to mask the roar of an aircraft as large as a Hercules dropping out of the sky.

When we landed the first thing I needed was fags as I had run out in Qatar. I could see a little shop inside the arrivals lounge so I grabbed my luggage and ran over quickly before we were called in. My first impression of Basra airport was that it looked amazing. It was immaculate and the floor was highly polished marble, far more luxurious then anything I had seen in the UK. In the shop I found a young lad no older than 15 years of age running the place. The shop was filled with Iraq memorabilia, and of course, countless brands of fags. I asked the boy how much they cost and he said they were $7. Although this was Iraq, we used American currency which was great due to the exchange rate. It worked out at about £3.50 in British money whereas 20 fags back home cost more like £6.00.

"I'll have a pack of B&H please mate". To my surprise he threw me a pack of 200. I told him that I only wanted a pack of 20, only to be told that it was $7 for the whole carton of 200 cigarettes. I couldn't believe it, what a bargain! I ended up buying 1000 right there and then.

Our call came over to get ready to move. Outside the airport there must have been about fifteen coaches waiting, so I grabbed my Lionel Richie CD from my holdall before chucking it back in the luggage space. I was pretty relaxed on the journey to SLB with Lionel's hits like "Penny Lover" and "Stuck on You" pumping into my ears.

We arrived at SLB at 01:00. We were absolutely knackered and wanted to get our heads down, but there was a load of admin to carry out first. It was 04:00 before we finally got to bed. Waking up the next morning, the sun was shining and we were given a tour of the camp. The place was huge with thousands of troops based there. It served as the main operations base for

A Soldier's Story **The | Battle | Within**

the south and was the Iraq version of Camp Bastion. Everyone would spend time here before they were deployed on the ground. It was relatively safe and secure and allowed us the chance to acclimatise before hitting the streets. There were shops to buy fags and other bits and pieces, as well as a large tent which contained the entertainment stuff like Sky TV, games consoles and telephones. Over the far side was the field hospital, a place I would be visiting in the not too distant future, although I didn't know it yet.

Conditions at SLB were pretty good but I was only there a few days before it was time to move on to our Forward Operations Base ("FOB"). My team's support company would be based at Az Zubbaur Port ("AZB"), Bravo Company was at Camp Chindt and Alpha Company at Al Amaran.

AZP was pretty basic. We stayed in a large air conditioned tent which was more like a sauna due to the broken air conditioning unit. There were ten beds to each tent with wash rooms and toilets close by. The heat was relentless, you could take a shower at 02:00 and walk back to the tent with just a towel around you. The heat radiated from your skin and you'd be completely dry after walking 60 feet or so.

The scoff house was just a stone's throw away and stocked with all the usual stuff we had back home. Hand hygiene was on top form as there were a number of anti-bacterial gel machines stationed at the entrance to the restaurant along with 10 gallon barrels of mineral water.

Our role while based at AZP was to help train the current Iraq police force. We were supported in our role by a member of the British Military Police and an Iraqi interpreter. It was more or less a 9 to 5 job with no night shifts required. Each morning we would have a quick kit check before loading up into two Snatch Land Rovers. We were given our plans for the day, a packed lunch and 6 litres of water that was issued to each man. We had a number of different police stations to visit throughout the day and just getting to each one was a risky task in itself. We always tried to change the route we took to the stations, as well as varying our arrival times. The terrorist groups knew we visited the stations during the day but we needed to keep them guessing. While we could change our route around the city, what we couldn't change was the route back to AZP.

There was only one way in and out of AZP. Unfortunately for us, the road was about a mile long with open ground on either side. It was a dangerous road but we had no other choice but to use it. During the drive out your arse cheeks would be so tight you could hold a penny between them. While the Land Rover would provide some protection against small arms fire, if we were hit by an RPG we would be done for, and in all honesty, a whopping great jeep isn't exactly the hardest target to hit.

Once we arrived at the police station we would quickly get ourselves into a solid, all round defensive position. Damo, Red Cap and the interpreter would spend an hour with the Iraqi police going over skills and drills. Some of the stations were right in the centre of the city and it felt like we needed eyes in the back of our heads if we were ever going to spot a real threat. There were hundreds of people who I thought looked dodgy, and the chances of spotting a car bomb were slim to none. The roads were packed with cars, bikes, and even donkeys. There was no sense of road management and everyone was treating the road as if it belonged to them. It was like the Arc De Triomphe but with less driving proficiency.

While we were providing protection, we daren't stand in the same spot for more than a few seconds. You just didn't know if anyone had you in their sights. As for the Iraqi police, the most professional thing about them was the way they maintained their patrol cars. They might as well have been brand new they were so shiny and dent free. It's a shame the same couldn't be said for the people driving them. They seemed far too laid back given the ever present risk of death that surrounded them. On several occasions I had seen loaded AK47's left in unlocked patrol cars while the officers disappeared into the station for a coffee or prayer. Pretty unbelievable. The condition of the cells was equally as bad. I'd seen a few with as many as ten people crammed into it. There were signs of human faeces up the walls and the place was buzzing with flies. It looked more like a torture box than a cell, I wouldn't have kept animals in conditions like that, let alone human beings. So far on the journeys between stations and the port, we had encountered very little drama. I can only remember one time when I thought it was really going to kick off, and that was while I was on top cover in the Land Rover. We were making our way through some back streets when a young child no older than 10 years old started shouting "Ali Baba… Ali Baba!" and pointing

A Soldier's Story **The | Battle | Within**

down the road in the direction we were headed. Ok, I thought, time to get ready for a contact. If they RPG us though, we were finished. Thankfully, it didn't escalate any further that time. We might have been having a peaceful run around but word on the street was that Alpha Company were having a fair few battles up North in Al Amarah, and we often visited Bravo Company at Camp Chindt to lend a hand.

It was a decent sized camp for the company, with the Iraq Police Training Academy situated adjacent to it. Every morning a large number of police recruits made their way to the academy for their day's training. The training academy even had instructors from the Met teaching there.

It wasn't long before the decision was made for us to move from AZP to Camp Chindt. It was easier, safer, and less distance for us to travel each day. I was more thankful that I would be out of that sauna of a tent we had been staying in. We moved into our new accommodation late on a Tuesday evening and only had time to dump our kit before it was time for us to turn in for the night. Another busy day ahead tomorrow.

Chapter 05

Carnage

Wednesday 21st April

I woke up at 06:30 and it was already starting to warm up. Even at that time in the morning the temperature was in the high 60's. I thought it would turn out to be a good day, little was I aware of the danger looming in the distance. After getting dressed I went to the cook-house to get a fried breakfast down me, and chatted with the lads about our plans for the day, deliberating over which DVD we should watch that night. Our team leader Corporal Damon Hudson (we all called him "Damo") came in and said, "Lads, be outside the Ops room at 08:00 for a sitrep and a quick kit check". We were ready to go.

I returned to my room to sort my shit out, packing away all unnecessary kit and at 07:55 I stood outside the Ops room with Chris, Danny, and all the others, ready for our plans and kit check. Damo filled us in on the procedure we'd be following for the day and gave us a current sitrep before moving on to the kit check.

We had all our kit laid out in front of us as Damo started calling out the items. Body armour and 2 trauma plates, helmet, personal role radio (PRR), 10 rounds of 5.56 ammo, dog tags, 1 morphine auto injector, and a full CamelBak. This is when it all kicked off.

All of a sudden sounded the loudest noise I have ever heard, followed by a huge vibration through the ground. What the hell was that? I began grabbing rounds of ammo and stuffing them into my pockets, then along with the others I legged it into the building for cover while we waited for more information. I was loading magazines with ammo faster than ever before when a runner came in just as I was finishing putting the plates back into my armour.

"Reports are saying a suicide bomber has driven through the camp main entrance, we have a number of dead and many injured. Are there any medics here?"

"Yes" I said, "I'm a combat team medic."

Everyone in the British Army from pastry chef to paratrooper is trained in basic first aid as part of their recruit training, but a team medic undergoes a more advanced programme of an additional week. It covers areas such as gunshot wounds, broken bones, hot and cold injuries, and administration of IV drips and triage patents.

"Ok" he said, "grab your kit and follow me".

I stationed myself inside the compound as the injured were brought in, some by foot, some by Land Rover. The injuries were shocking as men soaked in blood with deep shrapnel wounds came into the building. I could see one bloke holding his hand in pain and called him over. He had lost part of his hand and fingers but I didn't have any proper medical kit with me apart from a load of FFDs (first field dressings are a highly absorbent sterile dressing with tape to secure it in place), all I could do was wrap the dressing around his hand as tightly as possible to reduce the blood loss.

My responsibilities changed when a big crowd of people began to gather outside the camp entrance. There were perhaps 100 or more who had heard the explosion from the village half a mile away and had come to see what had happened.

This was concerning the camp commanders as it made it much more likely that we would become a target for a second attack now there were more people here.

My team were given the task of dispersing them but it was going to be risky. We had a number of guys from B Company who were going to provide armed cover for us from within the compound, but being on foot outside the compound we would have little protection against a vehicle bomb.

As we advanced towards the camp entrance, we got down low and used the hesco bastions for protection. Hesco bastions are a type of military gabion which provides defence from explosions. They are usually filled with a heavy material like rubble or earth and are made from collapsible wire and heavy duty fabric. Lieutenant David Lake turned to us and said, "Right lads, 10m spacing and prepare yourselves for some graphic scenes". As soon as we started to run out, I could see what he meant about the graphic scenes. There were blood stains smeared along the walls, human body parts sprawled across the floor and brick walls reduced to rubble. The hesco bastions had shrapnel sticking out of them and some had even begun to fall apart. There were also the remains of the bomber's car against the wall. A car crusher couldn't have twisted the car's metal into the shapes the bomb had created, it was barely recognisable as a car except for the odd buckled wheel.

I was taking in the realities of the situation faster than a Pentium processor as I hurriedly made my way towards the assembling crowd. Tensions ran high as we formed our baseline spread out over a distance of 70 to 80 metres. Some of the horde were getting aggressive towards us with some of them throwing rocks, and I could feel the build-up of sweat starting to run down my forehead. I was the last man on the far left with Chris to my right and Lieutenant Lake the next man down.

An elderly Iraqi man approached me with tears in his eyes. He had two young children with him, a boy and girl no older than 9 or 10, and was desperate to get past me. Why? I didn't know, I couldn't understand him but thought perhaps his son was a member of the Iraqi police and was worried about his safety. I had my orders though, no one to break the line. I did allow him and the children to pass me, but only to sit on a rock to rest.

It had been an hour or so since the bombing and most of the crowd had left, leaving 30 or 40 people. Unbeknown to me, something else was about to happen.

I could hear a vehicle engine in the distance that sounded like it was high revving. I started scanning the ground ahead of me, where is it? What is it? I couldn't see anything but didn't need to wait long. All of a sudden a vehicle appeared from the buildings 200m away. Fuck, fuck, fuck… it was heading directly towards me. I lifted my rifle up and looked through my rear and front sights, I knew for sure that it was another suicide bomber. Could I hit it? Unlikely, I could barely even see the car as it bounced all over the place. Even if I did manage to hit it, it wouldn't make much difference because the bomber was going to die anyway and would carry on regardless of any injuries or damage to the vehicle I caused. Plus, it could have been remotely detonated anyway. In those few seconds I decided that time spent trying to shoot the car was time wasted.

My best bet was to try and get as much distance between myself and the bomber as quickly as possible. The only option I had was to go left, I could see what looked like a deep crater 40m away and it soon became a race against time. To make matters worse, I'd been having problems with my left knee recently which made running painful, but at that moment it didn't hurt at all. I started to sprint as fast as I could towards the ditch whilst trying to keep the bomber's location in the corner of my eye. I stopped a few metres short and looked over my right shoulder. I could see the car passing within 20ft of me and I thought I was safe.

At that moment, he detonated the bomb.

There was a colossal explosion followed by a feeling that can only be described as being hit in the back with a sledge hammer. Immediately after the deafening boom came an immense blast wave; a huge amount of pressure lifting me up and slamming me into the ditch. I lay face down with my rifle blown clean from my arms and the sling wrapped around my neck. I couldn't breathe, the impact had knocked the wind out of me completely, as if I'd just been rugby tackled by Jonah Lomu running flat out into me. My back was hurting and I wasn't sure if it was broken, though it bloody well felt like it was.

Chris called over on the radio, "Neil mate, you ok...?" I said, "Yes mate, but I think my back is broken". I tried getting to my feet and it was then that I noticed my arm. The blood was squirting out all over my clothes. My left forearm had been torn open by shrapnel and there were bits of flesh hanging out. When I saw the state of my arm I began to flap a bit and felt faint. I grabbed my FFD and tried my best to tear it open (The FFD has a sort of canvas packaging), but with only one arm working it looked like that wasn't going to happen. I needed help and quick, I was losing a lot of blood.

My ears were ringing and there was dust all around me. I wasn't sure if it was a good idea to try and run across the waste ground but I had no choice. I made a break for it grabbing my rifle in my right hand as I held the FFD between my teeth and ran towards Chris who had made it to another ditch. I gave him the FFD and showed him my arm. As he applied the dressing I could feel myself becoming weaker as shock started to take over. I'm not sure who it was, but someone came up behind me, lifted me up and said, "Run".

I headed towards the camp and company aid post and felt like a complete mess. My left knee was in agony, my back was pounding and sore, my left forearm was literally in pieces and I was caked in blood. Strangely, although my arm was by far the worst injury I had, it didn't hurt. It might have been the fact that all my nerve endings had been damaged, I'm not sure. It just felt heavy, really heavy.

The blast from the second bomb was powerful enough to completely blow the vehicle in two. It was this bomb that injured me.

As I neared the camp, I passed the bombers car. It had been blown into two parts and a male body was lying just a few feet away. No, it wasn't the bomber, it was a member of the crowd. He couldn't get out of the way fast enough and didn't stand a chance. I stopped to look at him. He had lost two limbs and part of his face, and was very badly burned. I remember thinking, "This chap was walking around only a few minutes ago and now look at him". It was an image I would remember for years to come.

I soon had two medics running out towards me and they helped get me to the company aid post. I lay on the floor with a pillow beneath my head and was jabbed in the leg with pain relief, good old morphine. There was another lad in the room being treated with me, Lance Corporal Wayne Williams, and he had taken shrapnel to the face. I wasn't sure how bad it was but the amount of bandaging on him showed it was more than just a nick. We made eye contact and I just gave a little nod.

I'm here with you brother.

The carnage from the first car bomb, barely recognizable as a car apart from the odd buckled wheel.

A Soldier's Story **The | Battle | Within**

The scene outside Camp Chindit following the first bomb attack. 3 dead bodies can be seen just inside the compound. It was this gathering crowd that myself and the rest of my team were sent to disperse.

Chapter 06

Bomb Proof

At last the morphine was starting to kick in and I was beginning to feel more relaxed. There was also a sense of euphoria that followed, feeling great happiness of at last conceding to my situation. My mind was racing. Holy shit. Did that really just happen? Stuff like that only seemed to happen in Hollywood movies. Although I was rather unhappy about my new chest rig being cut apart when I was being treated, I could always buy another one.

I was shepherded into a medical Land Rover which was taking me to the field hospital at SLB. My arm was now raised above and behind my head, out of my sight. Still I had no pain, just a deep ache and an immobile arm. Shit, I thought, my arm is dead. I asked the medic by the side of me how it looked and her reply was, "I'm no doctor but it sure looks nasty".

At the last minute it was deemed too risky to travel by road so a helicopter was ordered instead. I was happy with this, always a fan of flying. Within 10 minutes a Chinook arrived and landed just outside the back of the compound. I was rushed out and up into the air in no time, with the on-board medics monitoring me throughout the flight.

We arrived in what seemed like minutes and dropped down right outside the hospital entrance. I was taken out on a stretcher and left waiting behind the helicopter. The sun was shining but it was uncomfortable, I could feel the heat from the Chinook's turbines blowing towards me and my now wasted arm. I remember thinking, if this takes any longer they'll be treating me for burns as well.

After a few minutes of roasting in the heat, a team of medical staff took me into the hospital. There must have been about ten of them in all. They cut all of my clothes off me except for my boxer shorts, as they needed to check me all over for other injuries. A mask was put over my face and the next thing I know, I'm out cold.

I woke up about 4 hours later with a huge bandage on and feeling very sweaty. It was mid-afternoon by then and the temperature was in the high 40's. A friendly nurse came over and said, "Your parents have been informed of your condition and you'll be leaving on the next medical flight back to the UK". I knew my arm was bad but I didn't expect to be sent home. The nurse helped me to the showers to get cleaned up before my transport arrived. While in the shower I finally got to see what the blast had done to my back. It was black, a deep bruise now covering most of it. The bruising was most likely caused by my trauma plates; solid pieces of steel which are fitted into the front and back of your body armour to protect your heart.

After having a good scrub and feeling much fresher, I made my way to the TV room to see some of the news from back home and an hour later the transport came for me. There were four more injured lads coming back to the UK with me that night. We grabbed all of our kit and left to board the minibus waiting for us outside. The journey to the airport was slow and unnerving as we passed the many VCP's along the route. We travelled under armed escort with military Land Rovers to the front and rear, filled with guys armed to the teeth, on guard for any potential threat towards our soft skinned minibus. However, I was unarmed, and even if I did only have the use of one arm, I still would've felt safer if I'd have had a firearm on me. You know, just in case. Each vehicle coming towards us put me on edge. After all, the last vehicle I saw heading in my direction only 12 hours before had nearly blown me to bits. Despite my apprehension, we made it to the airport without any difficulties and straight away I was made to feel at home. We were housed in a building on the side of the airport in an old aircraft hangar. There was tea, coffee, hundreds of DVD's to watch and we also had the use of a satellite phone to contact family and friends. We were then informed we would be leaving later on that evening.

I called my mother who told me the military had contacted her shortly after the bombing to tell her that a few members of the regiment including me had been injured, but they weren't told much more at that point. She also said that the bombing had made the front page of the South Wales Argus, our local newspaper. She supplied them with an old photo of me, along with what little information she'd been given about what happened. After our conversation I got some food down me while I waited for the flight.

Due to undisclosed reasons the flight was going to be delayed by 48 hours. The real reason was because of the appalling availability record and repeated break-downs of RAF aircraft. So, all we could do was make use of the services on offer to pass the time. I lost count of the number of films I watched, most of which, surprisingly, were war films, my favourite being "Saving Private Ryan". Two days later the plane was all set and I was strapped into the RAF Hercules aeromed flight for the 8 hour trip to Brize Norton. From there a minibus would take us to hospital.

It was a good job I was shattered as there was no entertainment on the flight and the only view I had was of the ceiling. I was secured to the bed like something from Silence of the Lambs with only a nurse popping back and forth for company. I must've fallen asleep before we got to maximum altitude because the next thing I remember is being woken up just before the start of our descent. The flight had at least given me some much needed rest. Clutching our kit, we saw the minibus waiting for us outside.

We were being taken to Selly Oak hospital in Birmingham which has now closed down, but back then Selly Oak was home to the Royal Centre for Defence Medicine ("RCDM") and they had an entire ward dedicated to treating injured service members. It was also one of the best trauma hospitals in Britain at the time. There were people there with just about every battle injury you could think of. From gunshot and shrapnel wounds to burns and amputations, this place had seen it all. It's no surprise that many army medics spent time here before deployment to conflict zones; they could gain the most paramount of experience.

My parents were at the hospital by the time I arrived and I was given a bed straight away. A nurse told me I'd be going into theatre later that day and she wanted to change my bandage now. "Yes, that's fine" I said. It was starting to smell a bit by this point. What should have taken about 10 minutes ended up taking nearly an hour. The nurse tried to remove the dressing but it was too painful so she gave me a shot of morphine and soaked the bandage in water for 20 minutes. She came back a bit later and started to cut through the layers of cloth. The last few were unbearable and I asked her to stop.

"It has to come off Neil."
"I'm well aware of that," I said, "but it hurts."

She disappeared and a new nurse turned up, a more senior one, and in one quick motion she ripped the bandage off. OUCH. I shit you not, I nearly hit her. What we didn't realise was that my arm had been left with an open wound, and as she was removing the dressing she was in fact pulling out the guts from inside my forearm. Due to the 48 hour delay of my flight, the blood had congealed and the tearing had re-opened my injury. Boy was it painful. Anyway, it had at last been changed and so I waited to be called for surgery.

I finally got taken down to be operated on and was out for only 2 hours. Apparently there was a problem. Because my arm had been left exposed it was now badly infected and the repair work couldn't go ahead. The surgeon removed the grit and shrapnel that was embedded in the wound and stitched my arm up. I was given a strong course of antibiotics to kill the infection and told it would be a few weeks before I could return for the repair work. My back was still bruised and sore but it would make a full recovery.

My arm however, was different. I ended up with 100% ulnar nerve and deep tissue damage. The ulnar nerve runs from the elbow through your arm and allows your little finger and ring finger to feel sensation. Both fingers were completely dead.

I hadn't yet been told when I could go home, so most of my time was spent outside in the smoking shelter talking to the other guys. I was a heavy smoker and could get though a good 40 fags a day, which also meant forty trips in the lift. I could've used the stairs but I was still connected to an IV drip. Talking to the other lads we traded stories. You could tell that many of these men were deeply traumatised by their experiences, and I couldn't blame them. One lad I was talking to had been in the back of an APC when it was hit by an RPG. He had taken quite an impact and most of the shrapnel as well by the look of him. He must have been about 5lb heavier with all the staples holding his body together. There was a boy in the bed opposite me, he was 19 years old and had taken a 7.62 round from an AK, straight into his forearm. Believe me, the lad was in pain and there was little flesh left on the bone. One thing was for sure, many of these soldiers' lives would change forever, some for the better. Most for the worst.

After 4 days of bumming around, I was told I was well enough to go home and could be released into my parent's care to recover at home. I was then placed on long term sick leave by the military doctors. My uncle was also on his way up to visit me which was great, and even better, once he arrived I would be going back with him. After packing up my kit bag and saying my farewells to the lads and hospital staff, I got in the car and headed for home.

I had never before been so happy to see the sign, "Welcome to Wales". As soon as I returned home, friends and neighbours popped in to see me and it was great to see everyone, but what I really wanted was a nice cold pint of Guinness. I hadn't had one since the night before leaving for Iraq and it was something I was very much looking forward to.

The Chinook helicopter carrying the (MERT) Medical emergency response team at camp Chindit, waiting to take me to the field hospital at SLB.

Chapter 07

Lost In The System

For the first couple of days back in the UK, I mooched around the house. I spent wasted hours browsing the internet looking at random stuff or getting in my mother's way while I waited for the pub to open. Then I would disappear until dark.

I wasn't drinking heavily but made sure I paced my consumption to fill the day and keep myself occupied. It was a coping mechanism, my way of dealing with the stress of the bombing and my now large surplus of time. I used to play darts years before joining the Army, and being sat in the pub all day I quickly took it up again. I played all day from the time they opened until 21:00, stopping at 13:00 for lunch – a juicy 8oz steak complete with all the trimmings. This became my routine, exactly the same every day like clockwork.

The South Wales Argus was keen to hear my side of the story so a reporter and photographer were sent to interview me.

The article made front page news and began to attract a great deal of attention. Before long, the BBC got in touch. Radio Wales and Radio 5 Live also wanted to meet me and do an interview about the bombing, which wasn't a problem, however Radio 5 Live wanted to do the interview from my home. They set-up a huge satellite dish in the back garden, the neighbours must have thought we were trying to recreate a scene from the film ET.

Aside from the dish another issue was that because this was going out live, I needed to be careful because I didn't want to be responsible for breaking operational security or the Official Secrets Act. They told me the interview would last no more than 10 minutes and I would be asked some questions about the bombing and what daily life was like on the ground in Iraq. They were also interviewing former SAS soldier and best-selling author Andy McNab about his new book and as soon as his interview was over it would be my turn. The questions ranged from how I felt about the war to how the locals treated us, and of course, a number of inquisitions on the bombing itself. After the interview I was given a taped copy as a keepsake.

Exactly one week after the bombing I decided to venture out into the city nightlife. With hindsight it wasn't the best idea given my physical condition, but it wasn't as if I was going out on my own.

I'd had a good few Jack Daniels' by the time we headed into town, taking in a few of the bars along the way before ending up in the city's main hotspot. My friends and I entered the club, drinks in hand and having a good time.

Dave had gone to get the next round in when without warning, I felt an unexpected blow. Out of nowhere some little shit had punched me clean in the face and then vanished into the throng of the club. I could feel the blood dripping down my chin, I had to leave.

Whilst trying to get out of the packed club I bumped into Dave, drinks slopping about. "What the hell happened?" he asked. "Long story I'll tell you tomorrow" I replied as I made my way out and disappeared to go home.

The blood kept flowing so I stopped at a kebab shop and grabbed a wad of serviettes to plug the wound.

When I got home I could see the damage; my top lip was split open. A long time ago as a young boy I had been bitten on the face by a German Shepherd, leaving two slice marks in my lip. The bite had healed well, but this punch had opened up the old scar and it was clear that a trip to A&E was needed.

On arriving in A&E it was evident that the weekend was in full swing. The place was packed with drunks full of bravado that intoxication often brings. These booze fuelled idiots masquerading as tough guys must have made the hospital a nightmare for the staff. After a quick check-in with the triage nurse and labelled as "walking wounded", I took a seat and waited to be seen, getting all the entertainment I needed to pass the time from the drunken louts littered about the waiting room. An hour later a nurse called me into a cubicle, the look on her face when she saw me was a picture. I looked a right mess. My nice crisp white shirt was now covered in a mixture of Guinness and blood, my top lip was sliced open and my left arm had a thick bandage on it.

"What on earth has happened to you?" She asked.

"I was punched in a club an hour ago" although she had probably worked that out for herself. What was puzzling her was my arm.

"What about your arm?"

"Oh," I replied, "I was blown up in Iraq last week." To be honest I'm not sure if she wanted to laugh or cry, but I'm certain that our exchange would have stuck with her and made her shift a change from the usual happenings found in A&E on the weekend.

The nurse did a great job repairing my lip and I was soon back in action. The next few days were pretty much as before, with days spent at the pub in my usual routine. Ten days after the bombing, letters of best wishes started to arrive from my mates still out on the ground in Iraq. I also received a card full of messages from the lads. One, from a good friend Paul Baston, read: "All the best Spence, that's one war wound to add to the many more to come."

It was a welcome reminder of the great, yet darkly tinged humour shared by those in the forces. Included in the well wishes were some letters from my company commander Major Lock.

There were two letters, one addressed to me, the other to my parents. The letters outlined exactly what had happened that day and how proud he was of the men under his command. The thing is, I could remember exactly what happened that day, it was so fresh in my mind that I could taste it.

It hit home that I still hadn't had any information regarding trauma management or physiotherapy. The following week, still with no word and being a glutton for punishment I went back to the club, only this time I ended up being the aggressor. I was on the bottom dance floor alone and quite drunk, when another drunken lad knocked into me and clipped my bad arm. I instantly lost control and found myself grabbing him around the throat before tripping him up. Before anything else could happen, four burly doormen grabbed me and ejected me from the club. I found myself sat on the curb alone, and started to cry. I didn't understand what or why, but something inside me had changed.

Another month passed without any information regarding my physio or trauma care. I didn't suffer from nightmares or flashbacks but it would've been nice to have been offered the support I might have needed. The BBC got in touch with me as they were running a documentary series called "Real Story" with Fiona Bruce. The episode was entitled "Coming Home" and examined the provision of treatment for wounded service members returning from Iraq and Afghanistan. Because my aftercare package had failed I was invited to appear on the show, and after meeting with the recording team and doing some fancy editing, the episode was aired in November.

A few months after the bombing while out in town drinking, I met a woman called Maria. She was the same age as me and lived on a nearby estate. We hit it off straight away. I might have still been drinking daily but instead of being at the pub, my time was now spent with her. Maria worked at a local electronics factory near Cwmbran and I spent every night I could at her place. She left the house every morning at 07:00 and wouldn't get home until 16:30, so when she went to work I would catch the 06:55 bus from

Bettws to Newport city centre. Each morning without fail, I bought breakfast and a coffee from McDonalds before walking to my parents' house where I would stay until Maria finished work.

One night while at Maria's, I received a phone call to say I was AWOL from my regiment and that if I didn't return by midday the next day, the Military Police would be sent for me. I explained that I had been injured and was on long term sick leave, but as far as they were concerned they were just following orders.

Early the next morning and still only having the use of one arm, I dragged my kit to Newport Army careers office to get a rail warrant, and 2 hours later I arrived at North Camp station for the trip to Aldershot. From there it was a 3 mile walk to the regiment's barracks. As soon as I arrived I dumped my kit and made my way to see the Regimental Medical Officer ("RMO"). Needless to say, he was shocked that I had been ordered back given the condition I was in, and wrote out a sick note before sending me traipsing back home again.

Maria and I had been together for 10 weeks when I decided I should propose. Over the next few weeks I got some cash together and went to buy an engagement ring, intending to propose as soon as possible. I didn't want to rush things but I had no choice, my regiment were due to deploy to Cyprus for several years once they returned from Iraq and at that time the future of my military career was uncertain. If I stayed with my regiment while I was single, I would go alone, however, if I was married then marriage quarters could be arranged for me. If Maria said yes then the wedding would have to take place before the Cyprus deployment. After a night out, we finished off in our local Indian takeaway and I dropped down on one knee. She said yes.

I was ordered back to barracks and this time managed to stay a week, but only just. There was hardly anyone around so there wasn't much to do as my TV and PlayStation were still locked away. It was incredibly boring. I went to my room and found that a new lad had settled in, which was a bit of a shock. My personal belongings had been moved into the block upstairs and this lad had taken my space. I couldn't say anything to him, it wasn't his fault, it just happens from time to time. My new room was completely empty except for my MFO box sat in the corner. I opened it and right at the very top was my pair of desert combats, the ones I was wearing when I was hit. I suddenly felt angry, I couldn't believe what I was seeing. I don't know what came over me but I started to punch the hell out of the box.

Once I had calmed down a bit I took the clothing out to have a closer look. My shirt and trousers were cut into pieces and the blood stains were still very much visible. On the top left pocket of the shirt, my details were still clearly written:

P1 (priority 1) Casualty
Blood Group B+
M (Morphine) 09:55

Being stuck in camp was horrible, I was medically downgraded and the only thing I was allowed to do was breathe. I didn't want to be there on my own, I just wanted to be back at home with Maria.

The thing is, I was still in the military and therefore had to be in a military establishment. However, I had a plan to rectify that and visited the RSM to express my concerns. I asked if I could be posted at the Newport Armed Forces Career Office as it would be a win-win situation for me. The Army were still in control of what I did, but I'd only be working a few miles from home so it was perfect. The RSM agreed to my request and true to his word he made the necessary arrangements. After a quick phone call he sent me over to Regimental HQ to collect a rail warrant so that I could report to the careers office at 09:00 on Monday. It was brilliant news.

I arrived in smart rig on Monday morning to meet the recruiting team. There were four platoon sergeants working there; one representative for each of the four Welsh regiments including Sergeant Neil Williams from the Royal Welch Fusiliers. A Warrant Officer Class 2 (WO2) from the Royal Green Jackets was running the place and it was an enjoyable place to work. Most of the time I was out walking the streets of Newport city centre, handing out leaflets to anyone who looked close to enlistment age.

One morning just before leaving for the office, a brown envelope was delivered.

It was from the Army Personnel Centre in Glasgow, informing me that since my discharge from Selly Oak Hospital I had been under the command of Y List. The Y list was a unit for injured soldiers who aren't well enough to return to their parent units or are likely to be given medical discharge. They would have been responsible for all of my treatment and general well-being. This explained it. My lack of treatment and AWOL status now made sense. I was lost in the system.

Maria and I hosted our engagement party at The Dodger, with the wedding to follow not long after as it had to come together so quickly before Cyprus. I wanted to wear a No1 Dress blue military parade uniform but didn't have my own set as they were very rarely issued. I was going to have to beg, borrow or steal if I wanted to get married in a set.

Raglan Barracks was only a couple of miles away, and as I knew a few of the TA lads who worked there I thought I could ask whether there were any uniforms I could use. Unfortunately they didn't have a full uniform, though I did manage to come away with some trousers. Sergeant Williams was heading back to Aldershot in a few days and offered me a lift, with a bit of luck they would have some uniforms in camp. Thankfully they had the rest of the uniform, which was a relief, and one thing ticked off the to-do list.

Maria and I visited the church to book a date for our wedding. After going through the diary with the priest we settled on Saturday 18th June - just 10 weeks away. There were so many things to organise in such a short period of time, but Maria's mum kindly organised most of it. Over the next few weeks we had our banns read and enrolled in a marriage preparation course. Every Wednesday evening for 90 minutes, we went through the program with other couples preparing to tie the knot. It was all starting to come together. We even managed to book our honeymoon online at a bargain price of £500 each for 10 days all-inclusive in the Dominican Republic. It was all going so well.

A Soldier's Story

The | Battle | Within

It was 10 days before the wedding and while I was at Maria's house my father phoned me.

"Neil.... your mother collapsed today, she's in the hospital."

It was too late for me to see her now so I arranged a visit the following day. When I arrived she explained what had happened. My parents had spent the afternoon in town doing a bit of shopping and decided to pop into the pub for a quick drink before going home. While they were walking back, my mother's hip collapsed.

She was unsure what the problem was with her hip or how long she would be in hospital but from where I was standing I had my doubts as to whether she would be out in time for the wedding. My mother was determined to be there though. With everything in place it would be too late to cancel so I just had to hope and pray that it would turn out ok.

The next time I was at the careers office I asked if I could finish a week before the wedding as I still had a few things to do. Sergeant Williams checked with the RSM back at Aldershot and it was approved. I went to the hospital the same day and my mother told me that her hip had snapped due to suspected osteoporosis. There was no way she would be out in time for the wedding, it was a huge disappointment now that it was so close.

Two days before the wedding I heard a knock at the door, it was Sergeant Neil Williams and he had come bearing gifts. He'd polished up a pair of ammo parade boots for me to wear, they were so highly polished you could've seen a spot on your face when you looked into them. I hadn't asked for the boots, it was just a kind gesture on his part and very thoughtful of him. The night before the wedding I stayed at my mate's house having a few drinks, a curry, and watching some films.

The day of the wedding was bright and clear and you could sense that it was going to be a warm day. Sadly, my mother was still in hospital and had asked the doctors if she could be allowed to attend the wedding in a wheelchair. The request was declined but they did agree to let her leave the ward for some photos later in the day. As per the forecast, it turned out to be the hottest day of the year with temperatures reaching the low 80's and with my uniform on it felt a lot hotter. I still felt really smart in my uniform though, despite the fact that I didn't have a medal on display. The church service went smoothly and we had some lovely photos taken outside and at Belle Vue Park. Afterwards, we went to visit my mother in hospital where a nurse had helped her get into the dress she'd bought for the special day, and she was allowed out on the hospital grounds to have some pictures taken. It was an uncomfortable situation as I was both happy to have her taking part in the proceedings, but sad that she couldn't enjoy the whole day with us. You could see the sadness in my mother's eyes as she missed her only son's wedding, she would've done whatever it took to be at the church, but what the doctor says, goes.

The whole day went according to plan and we were soon jetting off on our honeymoon, which was incredible. My mother was never far from my thoughts and as soon as we arrived I got hold of a calling card to ring home and find out how she was doing.

The Dominican Republic was a great experience with amazing weather and soft sandy beaches, there was so much for us to do including a vast array of water sports. When we finally returned home my mother was still in hospital, altogether she was there for 5 weeks.

It wasn't long before I moved out of my parents' house and into Maria's home with her mother and brother. I wanted to give my own parents some space as they needed it now my mother had been discharged from hospital. My father shifted the bed downstairs and the council installed a ramp in the rear garden so that my mother could enjoy some time out there. It must have been a difficult experience for my father juggling the care of my mother as well as trying to keep his business going.

I was invited to attend a medical board assessment to decide the outcome of my military career. My mind was all over the place and I was under a lot of peer pressure from family and friends who thought it would be for the best if I left the Army, and I could see where they were coming from. Firstly, I had been blown up by a bomb and I might not be so lucky next time. Secondly, my mother's health at the time meant that the family could do without any more bad news, and thirdly it was looking unlikely that I would be returning to my previous military role. I was heading towards more of a desk job and I knew that wasn't for me. I told the medical board about my family situation and my current feelings towards the military. I didn't want to work behind a desk and if I did remain in service then I wanted to go back into a combat role. Ultimately, I left the decision in their hands.

In the meantime, life continued as before. I was still working in the career's office and Maria had started working at the chip shop in the city centre. I also found out that my mother didn't have osteoporosis, it was much worse. The cancer had come back and this time it was terminal. Doctors informed us that she would be starting treatment shortly, but true to form, more bad news was on the way. It was early evening when my father phoned to say that my mother was being taken to St. Anne's, a hospice located a few miles away. I should point out that I really didn't understand much about cancer, I saw it as more of a treatable illness than a deadly disease

On Wednesday the next day, I took a trip up to see her. I grabbed some magazines from the shop on the way there, things like "Take a break" and "Bella" were her favourite, hoping that at least this would keep her occupied until it was time for her to come home.

She seemed ok, conceding to the situation and telling me she was going to hospital on Friday for her medication. I left St Anne's trying to remain as positive as she was.

Early Saturday morning my father phoned telling me to get to the hospice as soon as possible. Maria and I got there within 20 minutes. My mother's condition had deteriorated dramatically and I was told that she was unlikely to last the day. I was confused, I thought she was getting better. It turns out that my father thought it would be better to keep the real situation hidden, and now I could understand why. I wanted to go into the room to see her but I had a bad chest infection at the time so I asked the nurse if they had a mask I could put on, as I didn't want to pass my germs to my mother and make things worse. I was told to go right in.

Other members of my family were dotted around the room while my mother slept soundly due to the amount of medication she was on. She looked so incredibly weak and fragile, she must have been half the weight she was just a few days before and the colour had drained from her skin, leaving her sallow faced. I asked my grandmother when was she likely to wake up only to be told that she wouldn't. At that point I broke down, this was it, now it was just a matter of time. I wondered if she could hear what we were saying, I don't know if she could.

My sister and brother-in-law would want to be here too, but they weren't answering their phones. My father asked me and Maria to go quickly to Bettws and bring them back so my auntie gave us a lift. We finally managed to get hold of them but by the time we got back it was too late. We ran though the hospice entrance when my uncle Dave came over, his face giving away the reality of the situation. She was gone. I felt like I'd just been hit in the face with a brick. Dizzy and weak, I couldn't even cry. The feeling was horrendous and my mind was in overdrive.

The whole family spent 20 minutes in the hospice chapel in total silence, just enough time to take in what was happening. Straight after, I went outside with Maria for a smoke. My grandmother came over and said that she thought Maria and I should move back in with my father that night as he would need the company. The suggestion riled me a bit. It wasn't about the need to look after my father but why we had to be the ones to move in.

I was acutely aware that I already had enough of my own problems what with the bombing and my military career as well as my new marriage. I knew that I wasn't in the right frame of mind to be put in this position and I was pissed off that my sister and her family could more or less carry on with their lives without the added stress that I was now faced with. In spite of my feelings however, we moved back in that night.

A Soldier's Story **The | Battle | Within**

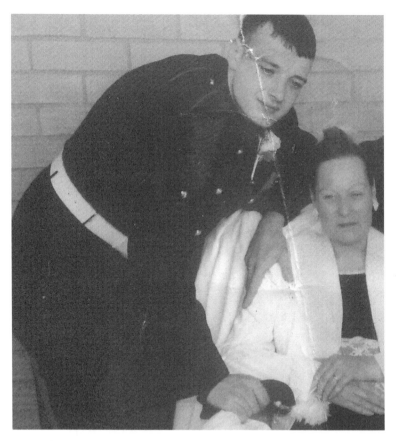

My wedding day June 2005, the last photograph I had taken with my mother. She passed away only 15 weeks later.

Chapter 08

Grief

As soon as we returned home I went next door to tell the neighbours the sad news. The lady and her family had been good friends with my mother for over 20 years, it was distressing for everyone who knew her.

The next day my father, Maria and I, didn't have a clue what to do with ourselves, it was almost like it were a dream - it couldn't be real, but it was. The TV was never turned on, just the music player. The music playing at the time was by one of my mother's favourite singers, Barry Manilow. The album was played repeatedly over and over and over again. I didn't like the music but my mother did. She used to play his album day in, day out and I guess my father must have felt like she was still around when the music was playing. I thought, well if it helps him then by all means let it play.

My father found the whole grieving process to be tough. It wasn't just the traumatic experience of losing his wife, but he also had the financial pressure of being self-employed.

As well as having to take time off work to care for my mother while she was ill, he was also trying his best to hold his business together. Most people struggle to do one of those things let alone both at the same time, but my father was - and still is - a strong man.

Furthermore, we had the funeral to think about. My father sorted out the funeral directors and the church service and I was given the option to go and visit my mother at the funeral home. I wasn't too keen on the idea at first but I knew I had to do it. It was a horrible experience seeing her lying there in an open coffin. She looked at peace and had been gracefully dressed, but it was still something I never wanted to see.

On the morning of the funeral I was running around like a headless chicken making sure we had all the food sorted for the wake. There was a knock on the door and I opened it to find Carol, the owner of The Dodger pub. She had the boot of her car full of food all readily prepared for us. It was a true act of kindness and I was touched by her compassion. The funeral took place at St John's Church, the same church my parents got married in many years before. The church was packed and there was a huge mixture of people my mother had known, a group of Asian lads who lived in the community even came to the service to pay their respects.

When the funeral was over there was a lot of tension hanging in the air. The TV was still off, with only the music in the background to mingle with the strain everyone was feeling. Both myself and my father were stressed out, it had been a rough few months, even years, and slowly we were starting to clash. I've lost count of the number of arguments we had and it was the last thing we wanted at that particular moment.

After 5 weeks I had had enough, I didn't want any more rows and it was time Maria and I had a place of our own. We took a trip bright and early to the council housing office to see what our options were. After an hour of waiting we were finally called in for a chat. I knew that if I was totally honest about living with my father then the chance of us getting a house or flat would be zero. I basically told the housing officer that I was ex-military and now homeless (at least the first part was true).

After what seemed like hours, we were offered a place at a homeless shelter until a property became available. Of course I rejected this, I couldn't take up a spot in a shelter whilst knowing there were genuinely homeless people who needed it more than me. Once we completed the paperwork it was just a waiting game. I remember thinking, as soon as I'm presented with their first offer, I'll take it.

That evening at home we didn't mention anything to my father about our plans to leave, I just thought it would be better to play it by ear. It was only 2 weeks later when the council contacted us.

"Mr Spencer? We have a property that has become available if you're still interested?" Damn right I was still interested!
"Ok, well, it's only a 1-bedroom flat in Bettws…" she said.
"What road is it on?" I asked, excited.
"Leach Road." Maria was thrilled as it was barely 300m from her mother's house, we would be mad to turn it down.
"You can view the property tomorrow if you like."

From the outside it was no oil painting, and the interior wasn't much different, but it was our own place and it's what we made of it that counts. The housing officer went through the terms and conditions of the property and showed us the inventory. She then informed us that pets weren't allowed. No pets? Damn. She hadn't mentioned it before. I'll just 'forget' to mention my dog Jasper… The council gave us a voucher worth £60 so we could decorate the place, but there was a catch. It could only be used in one store in town which had very little in the way of quality items. Tins of paint for £2 and rolls of wallpaper for £3, you wouldn't find any of your Laura Ashley quality in that place.

Armed with my new tins of paint and multiple rolls of wallpaper, I was looking forward to getting stuck in and making the house our home. I had never put up wallpaper before so it was a learning curve, and I actually surprised myself. Ok so there were a few bubbles hiding underneath once the wallpaper was up, but they soon dispersed overnight.

With the painting done and the walls covered, next to come was the furniture which came in the shape of several flat packs from Argos and left me £450 lighter in the pocket.

This was going to be another learn-as-you-go job as I'd never put one together before. Two hours later and with the help of a power drill, it was all assembled. Some people might hate flat packs, but I started looking for more to build.

We had been in the flat for a few weeks when a letter came through the door. It was addressed to me with a military stamp on the front and had been sent from my old regiment. I was being invited to a medal parade and a ceremony to celebrate St David's day. It was going to take place on Tuesday 28th February as the regiment had decided to celebrate the national day early due to plans to merge with the Royal Regiment of Wales on the 1st March – which is the actual date of St David's Day. Once amalgamated they would become one regiment called The Royal Welsh. Therefore the 28th February 2006 would be the last official day in The Royal Welch Fusiliers' history.

Even though I had been out of the military for 2 months, I was invited to be part of the day's celebrations, and of course to receive my Iraq service medal with the rest of the regiment. I was told I could travel up the night before and stay in the barracks. This allowed me to have a few drinks with the lads in town the night before. Well, there was no way I was turning that down.

I decided to leave mid-afternoon as I could get to Aldershot by 15:00 and have plenty of time for a piss up with the boys. Maria was going to spend the night at her mum's with the dog because she didn't like to be alone in the flat. If you had seen the place you would understand why.

My mate John said I could crash in his room for the night, so I dumped my kit and had a quick shower before chucking on some fresh clothing and heading out for North camp. I loved it. It was also a break for Maria whilst giving me the chance to catch up with old friends. Something that is special within the military is that it doesn't matter how long it's been since you've seen each other, you just carry on from where you left off. After God knows how many pints and games of pool, we went back to barracks with kebabs in hand.

On the morning of the parade, I was up early and had a banging headache. I needed a shower and some painkillers. As I made my way towards the NAAFI, the Regiments' adjutant called me over. The adjutant is an officer who is usually the rank of Captain or Major, and assists the Commanding Officer with staff duties.

"Neil, I've been unable to locate your Iraq medal."
"Really sir? I'll come and take a look". I started rummaging through the box of medals but could find none with my name on it.
"Bloody hell!" This could only happen to me, I thought. The adjutant tried to reassure me.
"I will personally make sure your medal is delivered to your home address within the next 6 weeks Neil." I couldn't say any more to that.

During the parade I stood in line with the other lads who'd been wounded, or were receiving bravery awards. I was presented with someone else's medal for the purposes of the parade, but would have to return it afterwards. We spent the rest of the afternoon in the officer's mess drinking brandy and talking to the lads about their bravery awards. I must admit, I did feel a bit of envy. I felt I should have been given a bit of recognition. After all, I had run forwards to treat injured people without hesitation or care for my own safety. But here I was struggling to even get my basic deployment medal. I felt disgruntled by the whole thing and just wanted to go home.

At home, daily life began to improve a little. As Maria was working in the chippie, I would visit my father at work during the day. We didn't live together now and found that we argued much less. This was good, but deep down I still had a lot of unresolved issues. Something in me just never felt right. I didn't suffer from nightmares or flashbacks, but I always felt on edge like I was constantly waiting for something bad to happen. I was unsatisfied with nearly every aspect of my life. I had a chip on my shoulder, and became angry with life.

It had been over 6 weeks since the medal parade and still my medal hadn't turned up. I decided to give the medal office a ring to find out what was going on, and was told that no one from my regiment had applied for my medal and the case was closed.

A Soldier's Story   **The | Battle | Within**

"what the hell does that mean?" I asked.

"You have to apply for it yourself. I'll send some forms out to you" the lady said.

The forms arrived a week later and I had to fill in my life story. They wanted to know everything about me – name, Army number, dates of deployment. Every damn thing. I filled it out and sent it off.

I quickly received their response. "Sorry Mr Spencer, you don't qualify as you didn't meet the required deployment duration". Are they taking the piss? I replied stating that I had been medically evacuated after being injured in a bomb blast. A good number of weeks dragged by when finally, a little white box came through the post. I couldn't believe my luck, it was my Iraq medal. Except it wasn't. It didn't have my name on it but my father's initials. I couldn't believe how I was being let down so badly. I got back on the phone to the medal office to explain the error. "Sorry Mr Spencer, send it back and we will correct it". "Forget it, I've waited long enough for this one, I'll put up with it" I said.

More nonsense followed. My service leaver's book arrived, a big red book containing your service history and personal information. I was listed as having blue hair and brown eyes. Well that was clearly the wrong way around. My height and blood group were wrong, and under the section listing scars, it said "nil". Really? Did they forget about the shrapnel in my left forearm? As this was an official record of service, it added insult to injury.

My family were hit hard again when my grandfather passed away following a short fight with pancreatitis. I was very close to my grandfather and spent most of my weekends growing up with him, be it camping in Pendine, fishing, or walking his German Shepherd dogs. He was full of pride about my military service and always made photocopies of everything I did. His loss wasn't just hard on me, but my father too. In the space of 2 short years he had to deal with his son being blown up and almost killed, the death of his wife, and now his father. How he was still holding it together was beyond me

After my grandfather's passing, I became more aggressive. I was slowly losing everything that meant something to me, and I had no control over any of it.

The bedroom door was knocked clean off the hinges, and almost every wall had a hole in it. Straight after these violent outbursts I was filled with huge feelings of guilt. I'd sit in the corner and cry, unable to explain why or what had made me explode. I knew I needed help.

I began by going online to find other soldiers who had gone through similar things to me, and found that a great deal of them were suffering from Post-Traumatic Stress Disorder ("PTSD"). I didn't know much about the illness at the time but found that many of the soldiers suffering with PTSD had seen some horrific things and were experiencing a lot of the same symptoms I displayed. I noticed that a few of them had been in contact with a military charity called "Combat Stress", so I decided to investigate a bit further.

I checked the charity out online and after reading about them and what they did, it seemed like they were the people who might be able to help me. It took a while for me to build up the courage to get in touch with them because I was embarrassed about phoning up and admitting I had a problem I needed help with. Yes, I needed help for my mood swings and anger issues, but I didn't like to think of myself as having a mental health problem. It's those two words "Mental Health", it makes you feel like a nutter or psycho and to be labelled as either one was the last thing I wanted. My doctor had previously prescribed me the anti-depressant Citalopram, but I'd never taken a single tablet for the very same reason. I thought of anti-depressants as being for people who were mentally weak - another thing I didn't want to be labelled as.

After a few weeks I finally pulled myself together and got in touch with the charity. They sent out some papers for me to fill in like my basic personal information, my military service, how I felt day to day, stuff like that. It also had to be signed by my doctor. I completed the form and posted it off right away.

An area welfare officer made contact with me a couple of weeks later, and asked when I was free to have a chat with him. I said I was available at any time and a week later he came to see me at home. He was a former military man in his 50's, well aware of the countless problems that ex-service members face. The conversation started by going right back to the very beginning as he asked me about my childhood.

We moved through the different stages of my life before progressing onto more recent matters and what had happened over the past 2 years. We talked for about 45 minutes during which he simply listened and took notes while I spoke. It felt nice to talk to someone who listened and understood instead of giving me the usual negative response I'd been accustomed to getting from others.

Afterwards, we shook hands and he said he'd be in touch soon. "Here's my card, any problems just give me a ring". I felt as though a weight had been lifted from me, I wasn't fixed yet but I had made a start.

Sometime later I received a letter saying, "Dear Mr Neil Spencer, we have a space available for 1 week at our treatment centre in Newport, Shropshire. Please respond with your decision". They enclosed some documents for me to sign, including a consent form allowing them access to my medical records. I signed everything and immediately sent it back in the post.

I couldn't wait to get there but a few days before I was due to leave I started to panic. I had seen the film "One flew over the cuckoo's nest" a few years before and was beginning to think I would end up in the same situation. I envisioned myself going in with anxiety and coming out with a ton of mental health problems and a daily dose of drugs. Of course, this was all down to my twisted thinking at the time and it wasn't like that at all.

When the day arrived for me to go to the treatment centre I was looking forward to it as a whole, although I would really miss Maria whilst I was away as it would be the longest we had ever been apart. When I reached the centre a friendly care worker welcomed me and helped me check in before showing me to my room. Upon entering the room, the first thing I noticed was a Bible by the side of the bed. Is it that bad here that I need a Bible? I wasn't one to read books, let alone the bible. I just don't have the patience. I have never been religious as such but have always believed in a form of afterlife. I think as adults, in a time of need we will always seek help be it from family or friends, or if unfortunate enough not to have either, we will seek guidance from the big man in the sky. As for the whole "Heaven and Hell" debate, I very much doubt it. As I grow older and wiser and witness the pain and suffering of the many people in the world, I can't help but think if there is a God, where is he now? But without hope there is nothing.

However, I believe for sure that something happens when you pass. I've been witness to quite a few paranormal events since my mother passed away, events that are very difficult to explain away reasonably.

After unpacking my clothes I took a short walk around the centre to get more of a feel of the place. I couldn't believe the number of older veterans who were there and it soon became clear that even at the age of 27, I was one of the youngest people being treated. Most of the men were around 50 or 60 years old with some even older than that. Nearly all of the guys suffering from PTSD had served in Northern Ireland or the Falklands War.

The centre had a beautiful garden area with plenty of benches to relax on. While outside having a smoke I got talking to a chap who was a former platoon sergeant in the Parachute Regiment. He started telling me about his time in the Falklands and how the lasting mental scars had caused serious damage to his career and family life. The next thing I know, he breaks down into a sobbering wreck right in front of me. I didn't know what to say, what could I say? As a young fusilier I used to idolise platoon sergeants like they were God. They were the ones you turned to for experience, help or support, and yet here I was in a position to offer help.

I met another bloke who also served in Iraq. He was a bit older than me and most of his time there was spent in the field hospital, treating the injured. He had 6 hard months of service and when he returned he didn't have a mark on him. However, the experience affected him so much that he filled his bathtub with bleach and scrubbed at his skin until it was raw. He may have been physically fine but deep down he had some long lasting psychological issues.

There was an interesting chap who I never got the chance to speak to. He was a strong looking bloke who had served in the Royal Marines and the elite SBS, and he certainly looked the part. He was very quiet, stood over 6ft tall and had a tailored moustache. During the day I never saw him move from his preferred chair except to make coffee or go to the toilet. He would simply sit there watching TV all day. On my third day at the centre I noticed this SBS guy wasn't sat in his chair like he usually was. I asked some of the other lads where he was and they told me he was in his room where he would stay until he left in a few days' time. I thought this was odd behaviour until I found out why.

He lived alone in a bedsit somewhere down south and lived like a recluse. When he visited the treatment centre every 6 months for 2 weeks, he treated it like a holiday. It was his respite, his chance to taste what normal life felt like with people he could empathise with. He apparently found it too difficult to just up and leave the centre on the pre-arranged date to go back to his lonely bedsit, so instead he would gently reintegrate himself back into his regular mentality by spending the last few days at the centre as he would at home. Alone.

It was a good break for me too, I felt totally relaxed during my time at the centre and for the full week not a single drop of alcohol ever came close to touching my lips. Unfortunately, as was the same for everyone else, it was soon my time to leave and return to reality.

I packed up my belongings and bid farewell to the lads and welfare staff, just in time as Maria and my father were only a few minutes away. It was amazing to see them again and on the way home we popped into a country pub for a pint and a catch up. They wanted to know how the week had gone and if I felt any benefit from it. The answer was a confident yes. I didn't realise at the time that it was only a temporary fix. When asked if I would like to return I should have said yes. During that week I had time to focus solely on myself, de-stressing and talking through my problems while I had the breathing space to do so, but I was never going to be fixed in just one week. It could take months or even years before I got the full benefit of treatment. It was a mistake I would later come to regret.

Chapter 09

Hitting The Bottle

The frequency of our arguments escalated and soon Maria and I were fighting daily. We were both under massive strain but I also felt riddled with guilt. I had become so aggressive and angry I hated it, I hated myself. Maria was going on holiday soon with her mother and aunt to spend 2 weeks in Tenerife. I hoped that the time apart would give me some time to unwind and do some thinking.

The day Maria left for Tenerife I was upset but luckily I had Jasper, my trusty dog, for company. I didn't have much to do around the house so I often kept myself occupied by popping round to my father's workplace with the dog for a few hours. It was during one of these visits that I came up with the idea that I'd had enough of the marriage and as soon as Maria returned I would let her know how I was feeling. Now that I had come to this conclusion I became anxious. How would I tell her? What do I tell her?

Her uncle dropped them off at Bristol airport, so it was my turn to do the airport run for their arrival home. I set off early as I didn't want to be late.

I got there in plenty of time, not least due to the fact that the plane was running 30 minutes behind schedule. Before long I could see the passengers making their way through the arrivals lounge.

I watched Maria coming towards me and she looked great, wearing a pretty dress which showed off her lovely golden tan. She came running up to me and gave me a big hug, telling me how she had had a fab time but was looking forward to getting back home to spend time as a family with me and Jasper. Then she reached into her bag and pulled out a gift. It was a bottle of Aramis Life, my favourite aftershave. My heart sunk. I'd already made up my mind, but how on earth could I tell her how I feel now?

During the journey home I carried on normally as I didn't want to break the happy mood. Once we got back to Newport I dropped her mum and auntie off first and it was almost time for me to break the news. There was no easy way for me to do it; I had to come straight out with it. The moment we walked through the door, I asked her to sit down. No messing about, I came straight out with it.

"I don't think the marriage is working anymore," I said "we need to call it a day." She began crying almost instantly, asking me if this was really what I wanted and telling me she married me for life, but I was resolute.

The atmosphere changed immediately and I felt a huge load had been taken off my chest. Amidst all the thoughts going through my head, I didn't realise that this was only going to be a temporary change. Maria arranged to move back to her mother's house and told me that she would be gone by the time I finished work the next day. When I got back home the following day, I felt different. The flat was eerily quiet and I didn't like it. All of her clothes and personal belongings had been cleared out and the place looked bare, it didn't look like a family home anymore and I suddenly felt miserable and alone. The reality of my decision was beginning to sink in. What on earth was I thinking? Had I made a big mistake? What if I had messed up big time?

I'd already been blown up by a bomb, lost my military career, my mother and grandfather, and now I was adding my marriage to the list. It was madness, utter madness. There were a lot of underlying issues and things to work out, but I still had hope in reconciliation.

Anything is possible, I thought. Deep down I didn't really want to end our marriage but I felt so bad about the way I was behaving, I was destroying her life as well as my own and I thought it was better to end it before things got really bad. She also had the support of her mother and family, a network I would now be without, and it was dawning on me that dealing with everything on my own was going to hurt.

I was already drinking every day but now my stress levels were starting to go through the roof. My coping mechanism was to drink even more. Deep at the back of my mind I thought at any minute Maria would walk through the door and say, "Come on then, let's sort this mess out." But it obviously wasn't going to happen. I left messages on her mobile and house phone asking her to contact me as I had things to say, but I got no response. I was spiralling into an emotional wreck. I didn't want to go to work, but I had no choice. Even when I was there I couldn't think properly nor concentrate on the tasks at hand.

Five days after we separated, I got home and found a letter on the fireplace with some money. It was £60 from our joint bank account, Maria had withdrawn the balance and given it to me. I didn't care about the money, but the letter was different. I found it hard to read, it brought tears to my eyes and a lump firmly in my throat. It was a letter to say thank you for all the good times, along with the bad, that we had shared together and how sorry she was that it turned out this way. She also said how much of a struggle things had become for both of us, but no matter what happened, I would always have a special place in her heart.

I felt sick and empty. It suddenly registered with me that this was it, no going back. So I began to drink even more. I wasn't having whisky on my cornflakes or anything that extreme, but as soon as evening came, the bottle came out. Every night I went through at least 10 double whiskies, and the minute the weekend came around, my alcohol consumption intensified. I would go through half a bottle of scotch before I'd even leave the flat, and once I got to The Nightingale (the local pub) I would start guzzling down pints.

In truth, the bomb blast may not have killed me but if I wasn't careful, the resultant drinking might. Another big problem I had was that I wasn't eating properly. Some people when they are stressed might comfort eat, but I was the opposite.

I couldn't face food and the most I would get through was maybe 400 or 500 calories from Mars bars and microwaved junk food of some kind. Nothing substantial and certainly nothing of nutritional quality.

My bodyweight slowly began to drop but I didn't consider the possible damage I was doing to myself. Mentally I was falling into a dark place and I needed help, but on the outside people thought I was coping well. I was apparently doing a good job at covering the real effect all of this was having on me. My life was in absolute turmoil.

One evening I lost the plot. The large fish tank in the kitchen was playing up, the water heater was knackered and now the tropical fish were living in cooler water. I was particularly drunk as I got on the phone to Maria to inform her that she needed to sort the fish out or they would die. She couldn't do anything and fuming, I slammed the phone down and turned around to punch the door. Unfortunately, in my drunken state I missed the door completely and ended up punching the glass tank. My fist smashed straight through the glass and 100 litres of water cascaded onto the kitchen floor. I could hear the young couple yelling in the flat below as the water seeped through the ceiling and into their kitchen. It didn't take long for the bloke to come running upstairs to find out what had happened.

I opened my door for him and he stared at my kitchen which was in a hell of a mess, with tropical fish flapping about on the saturated floor. What the hell could I do now? I'd drunk nearly a full bottle of whisky so there was no way I could drive. I decided to fill the sink with warm water and hope the fish would survive. It didn't work and a few hours later they were dead.

I asked my father if I could stay with him for a while and he agreed. I also decided that it was probably for the best if I gave up my flat as there were too many bad memories connected to it. Staying with my dad helped me to take my mind off some of my problems, but like me, he likes a drop of the old Scottish tipple which could quickly become a problem. I stayed with him for 3 weeks, sleeping on the floor, and every couple of days I'd go back to the flat to check my post and make sure no one had broken in. My flat was now totally empty. My father's mate ran a removal company and he supplied me with some large cardboard boxes to pack up my stuff. I had it all sorted out within an hour.

My wooden bed was dismantled, together with the wardrobe, and the carpets were ripped up. To see it looking so bare was quite sobering, it was hard to imagine a family had lived there once.

It's the furniture and the company that makes the difference between a house and home and to have that difference so starkly emphasised was upsetting.

After 3 weeks with my father I had second thoughts about the flat. Maybe I could stay there, decorate it and try to make a fresh start. It was difficult moving back and although I had been away for a few weeks, I still felt mentally insecure. The evidence of this instability was evident on every door and most of the walls which were peppered with holes from where I had lashed out in moments of uncontrollable of anger. I didn't have the money to replace the doors, so a trip to B&Q for some filler was needed. I also got some cheap wall paper and my father got me a remnant of floor carpet for £100. It was starting to look more like a home again.

I was deeply depressed and unhappy. Yes, my flat was starting to look better, but the past still had a firm grip of me and wouldn't let go. I didn't have the motivation to do anything other than listen to music and drink whisky. My bed was still in pieces as I couldn't even be bothered to reassemble it; instead I chose to sleep on the mattress on the floor. I had curtains but no curtain rail as I had snapped it in half when I intended to move, so instead of buying another one I used a satellite cable to hold them up. As for gas and electric, I had some, but they were constantly on emergency credit. I didn't have any lights either as the bulbs had blown and I never replaced them, instead resorting to candles. Looking back on that time, I can see that it was insane, and it nearly cost me my life.

One Saturday night I arranged to meet my father for a few drinks in Caerleon. I'd been doing a bit of painting earlier on and needed a bath before leaving. I filled the bath and hopped in, not noticing that I had knocked a bottle of white spirit that had been perched on the side, into the bath with me. Diluted or not, I can assure you that on the more sensitive regions it hurt like hell. It felt like I had sprayed a bottle of deep heat over the area.

It was burning so badly that I had to sit in cold water for half an hour, and even when I finally got out it took 2 hours for the pain to subside.

The rest of the night didn't improve either as my wallet was stolen, along with £50 and my driving licence. When I got home I was very foolish, not to mention dangerous. With no functioning lights in my flat, I lit a candle and positioned it on top of a cardboard box. But as pissed as I was, I fell asleep not long after lighting it. When I woke up the next morning I spent 5 minutes walking around before I noticed the candle was still burning, yes, burning on top of a cardboard box, and if that wasn't stupid enough I had even left the window open. It would only have taken a slight gust of wind to blow the candle over and the whole place would have gone up in flames with me inside, unconscious after the hammering I'd given my liver.

Although I was still drinking a large amount, something happened to me mentally that forced me to stop. I became a hypochondriac, someone who abnormally worries about their health, so much so that it becomes a form of paranoia. It was a side effect of the high levels of anxiety I was under. I became convinced that I had developed liver disease from all the heavy drinking, and found that I was regularly checking my skin and eyes to see if I had the yellow signs of jaundice. Every time I looked in the mirror all I could see was a yellow person looking back at me. Of course my skin and eyes were not yellow in reality, it was just my brain playing tricks on me. The human mind is so powerful that if you fixate so resolutely on something, in time it becomes very real.

The fear of the damage I was doing quickly forced me to stop drinking and seek medical help for my possible liver damage. I went to see the doctor for an emergency appointment and waited 2 hours to be seen. There was no way I was waiting 6 weeks for an appointment, the 2-hour wait was bad enough. The doctor asked me about my current psychological state and how much I was drinking. He gave me a piece of paper and told me to write down what I would typically drink during an ordinary week. The results were frightening. I was advised that the "safe" limits were up to 28 units per week or about 14 pints. Whereas I was consuming around 120 to 150 units, equivalent to between 60 and 70 pints a week. I agree that I was drinking a lot but because I was drinking the units in whisky, it didn't seem that much to me.

The doctor said I'd need a liver function test to check if there was any damage and if so, how bad it was. I knew this would send my anxiety through the roof as I'd have to wait a week for the results.

For the next 7 days I feared the worst. Terrible thoughts plagued me, but worst of all was knowing that if I was headed to an early grave, it was all my own doing. After 10 days I couldn't wait any longer, I needed to know. I dialled the doctor's number and was given the results. I couldn't believe it. Amazingly the tests came back showing that my liver function was not quite what it should be, but that there was no real cause for concern.

Even though I now had my results, I wasn't convinced. After all I was now a hypochondriac, I could never be convinced. Maybe the tests were wrong, or maybe the doctor was lying. What if I was dying? I decided to wait a week and then go back for more tests. I didn't even make it that long. I went straight back to see the doctor without the 7-day wait. The doctor tried his best to reassure me, explaining that they had completed 6 tests and only one had come back slightly raised. He advised me again to cut down on the alcohol and said I would be fine. He also gave me a prescription for the anti-depressant medication Citalopram.

I was a shadow of my former self. It was coming up to 6 months since Maria and I had split up and I was suffering from depression. My bodyweight was a shade over 10 stone, which compared to my usual 13 stone, made me look skinny and weak. It's difficult to explain just how alone you feel and how the isolation creeps in. I was under constant criticism from family and friends, I guess they didn't really have any idea of what troubles I had actually faced, but it just added to my resentment.

As Christmas approached I tried my best to get into the festive spirit. I propped a tree in the corner and because my liver results were fine I started to drink again. My fridge was bare with the exception of a few cans of lager. I also had a couple of bottles of whisky and some Irish Meadow, which was a cut price Baileys substitute. I honestly expected Maria to drop a Christmas card through the door, but nothing came. It turned out to be the worst Christmas day I've ever had. I ate dinner at my sister's before going back to my grandmother's with my father for a couple of drinks. It was that bad that by 6pm I was on the sofa bed ready to sleep. Time rolled on and by mid-January I felt that on the whole, my life was shit and was going to remain that way.

Chapter 10

A Fresh Start

During one of my regular nights out in the city I met a girl. Why she wanted to talk to me though, God only knows. I was skinny, weighed 10 stone soaking wet, and had more than a couple of screws loose. I caught sight of her sitting outside in the pub garden with her friends, so I walked over and started chatting to her. I can't remember what I said, if it was good or bad, but her friends stayed with her. I couldn't have been that charismatic as I ended up going home alone.

Two weeks later after a night out drinking a lot more than I care to think about, I staggered towards the taxi rank for a ride home. While I was waiting I bumped into the same girl from 2 weeks before, again out with her friends. One of her friends recognised me and I heard her whisper, "Look over there, it's that dickhead you were talking to the other week."

Dickhead, well that's a first. The girl came over to me and we talked for about 15 minutes, this time I managed to get her name, Selina.

Just before she jumped into a taxi I asked her if we could meet up again. She said yes, and handed me her phone number.

I gave her a ring the next day and asked if she fancied meeting up. She agreed and said to meet her after work on Monday afternoon, at the time she worked for BT in customer services. I was parked up outside McDonalds on the high street when Selina came to meet me. We went to a pub just outside Bettws and spent a bit of time getting to know each other. I also wanted to show her my flat, not that it was a palace, but it was my own place. She was hesitant at first, but then agreed as long as I dropped her back home later in the evening.

I don't think she was impressed with the flat. In all honesty, it was a shithole. I didn't even have a proper bed put together. My satellite cable was still holding the curtains up and I didn't even have a sofa to sit on - I was using a green council recycling box when I wasn't sat on the floor.

Selina lived with her parents in St. Brides which was on the other side of Newport. She had not long come out of a long term relationship herself and had moved back home until she got back on her feet. It seemed we had something in common there. As promised, I dropped her back home that night, and it wasn't long before she had moved in with me.

I personally wasn't keen on jumping straight into another relationship, especially after the last one had almost driven me to the point of suicide. For all my reservations though, I couldn't deny that it was nice to have company.

Over the next few weeks, Selina started to treat the flat as her own. She would come home from work with curtain rails, picture frames and other little bits to tidy the place up. It felt like life was starting to pick up again. She left BT and started working in the night at her family's fish bar in Magor, while I began working for a friend who was a butcher. I was the delivery driver and spent 7 hours a day dropping off meat to pubs and nursing homes within a 60-mile radius.

Now that Selina was living with me, the amount I was drinking dropped dramatically. I even quit smoking and started to do a bit of running around the estate.

One day Selina went and did a full weeks' food shop in Asda. The cupboards, fridge and freezer were full for the first time in ages. I loved it. There was so much choice. When I lived alone I hardly ever ate anything and even when I did, it was whatever I could get from the local Spar. Things were definitely looking up.

After we'd been together for a year we decided to get a dog. Selina wanted some tiny ankle biter but I wanted a German Shepherd, a breed I loved, having grown up with them. After much debate Selina let me have my way, German Shepherd it was. We began by looking through the free-ads and after a few weeks found a promising advert. There was a mixture of six dogs; 4 males and 2 bitches. They were 10 weeks old from a KC registered breeder based in Bettws, Bridgend.

We had a limited window of time to get to the breeder and see the dogs but we were really keen to put down a deposit. I suppose we could've waited, but I was anxious not to miss this opportunity as puppies are often snapped up within hours. Selina was adamant there was no way we could make it to the dogs and get her back home in time for work. However, I'd recently gotten a BMW M3 EVO and reassured her, with a grin, that there was plenty of time. The breeder agreed to meet us at McArthur Glen Designer Outlet and when we arrived I instantly fell in love with the dog. We brought a puppy home with us and now had a family pet named Tara.

Having a dog really helped to balance out and stabilise my mood swings and depression. I can appreciate now why dogs are sometimes used to help those suffering from PTSD. While the dog made me feel relaxed, she also liked to cause trouble in the flat as she chewed through pretty much everything that Selina owned; expensive handbags, watches, the lot.

I soon lost my job as a delivery driver and was back to scraping money together wherever I could. I took the initiative to register myself as self-employed and started doing odd jobs alongside my father, small jobs like car seat repairs and fitting convertible hoods to cars. Meanwhile, Selina was now out of the fish bar and working for a large company in Cwmbran.

We plodded on for the next 9 months, making ends meet, until one day Selina told me she might be pregnant. A shop bought pregnancy test quickly confirmed her suspicions. I was both excited and worried by the thought of having a baby, but definitely more worried. We were living in a small flat with a big dog and I didn't even have a decent income behind me. When we went for an ultrasound scan it became all the more overwhelming. We were expecting twins. It was a massive shock and neither of us knew what to make of the news.

Thankfully we had some help from Selina's family with things like buying a cot and a car seat, but it was still rather costly. While I was tremendously happy about these little baby boys coming along, I was nonetheless worried about where we were going to live. The flat wasn't at all ideal, even with just myself, Selina and the dog living there, you could hardly swing a cat. With two added people it would be impossible. Not only the space, but the dog. While I loved Tara, I couldn't risk having a large dog and newborns in the same space. Potentially, all it would take was for her to move and the damage could be devastating. Despite this though, I didn't want to rehome Tara either.

Selina's mother owned a property in Newport and told us that once the tenants moved out, we could move in. It was a charming 2-bedroom new-build house in the Celtic Horizons part of Newport. The rent was almost twice as much as the flat but in return we acquired more than twice the space, including a back garden and a garage. It would be enormous in comparison to the flat.

I was looking forward to moving in, although I can't say I wasn't anxious at the prospect of giving up the security of my own place, even though we'd been together for 3 years and were having children. I had first hand experience over and over again that life can change for better or worse in the blink of an eye. If it did change for the worse, I would most likely end up on my arse living on the streets. I couldn't help but fall back into negative thinking as I'd had such a rough time in recent years.

As part of the moving process, I built a kennel for Tara because she would have to sleep in the garden. I bought a 6ft garden shed from B&Q and knocked 3ft off of it. I padded the whole thing out with foam and then carpeted the bottom. It looked really good and was well insulated and dry. When it was time to move our possessions in, we booked the dog into kennels. There was plenty to shift and with Selina 8 months pregnant, I was moving most of the heavy stuff on my own. Two days later I handed the keys to the flat back to the council. I was dreading their inspection and repair bills.

Three doors had to be replaced as well as fixing four large holes in the plasterboard walls. They were also likely to charge me for items I couldn't take with me. There was an old sofa we had bought, as well as a big wardrobe. I only had the use of a small van and couldn't fit them in. I can't remember how much the bill came to, but I do remember having to set up a payment plan to clear the balance.

Once we had moved our stuff in, it was time for me to collect the dog and bring her home.

I set about decorating the place, the living room first, followed by my future boys' nursery.

Although we were now in our new home, we didn't want visitors, mostly due to not actually owning a sofa. We had a 32" flat screen TV on the wall but all we had to sit on was a small beanbag. That was it. We managed to rectify that just before the boys were due and got hold of a nice sofa from Next, so that at last, we had something decent to sit on.

Selina was soon in hospital and the twins were finally on their way. The pregnancy had been a rough 9 months for us, more so for Selina. For at least half of her last trimester, Selina was an in-patient in hospital due to various problems caused by the deadly pre-eclampsia, a condition which gave her swollen legs and prompted her blood pressure to shoot up. After a long 11 hours in labour, Selina finally gave birth to our 2 boys; Nico and Fabio. It was without doubt the happiest day of my life, and one I will remember forever.

Despite everything that had happened to me, I had a lot to be grateful for. Not only did the birth of my boys make me feel like I had been re-born myself, but they gave me a reason to live again. I was determined to set a good example for them so that one day they would look up to me for support and guidance. I also had Selina to thank. If I hadn't met her, who knows where I'd be now. Probably dead given the lifestyle I was living at the time.

Shortly after the twins were born, we received worrying news. Doctors had detected a problem with Fabio's heart and more tests were needed to find out the problem.

With Fabio's condition now on our minds, we weren't able to enjoy our time at home as a family until the root cause had been identified. Selina remained in hospital, I was at home, and the dog was back in the kennels. We had decided to keep the dog there for a few days while Selina and the babies could settle in at home without the added strain of keeping a close eye on Tara. I was only allowed to visit the hospital during visiting hours, but always tried to stay a bit longer than they allowed so I could spend more time with Selina.

A few days had passed since the twins' birth and I was alone at home watching TV, when there was a knock at the door. It was my grandmother; she had come to congratulate us. She also said that she'd spoken to my father and they had both decided that I would get rid of the dog. I had already considered rehoming Tara myself, but if I did it would be my choice, no one else's.

I was well aware of the dangers of having a large dog around young children, after all, I had been bitten on the face as a child by a German Shepherd. Although it was just an accident, I know how easily it could happen. However, I am a very loyal person not just to other people but in every aspect of my life, be it a pet or a job. Hence why I had built the kennel and made it as warm and comfortable as possible.

Another thing which irritated me was the number of my family members who thought I was weak because I was upset about giving up my dog. I wonder if they would be so keen to give up their pets, I doubt it!

I knew that I had to re-home Tara because it wasn't safe to keep her in the house with newborns, but it wasn't fair to make her live in the garden 24/7 either. It was a decent sized garden covered with grass, but where she'd been running around, the grass had become chewed up, and after a week it looked more like a muddy pigsty. Regardless of coming to this decision myself, it didn't make it any easier when the time came to let her go.

A friend of Selina's mother had shown an interest in the dog, so I offered Tara to her. She accepted and we arranged to meet at the kennels the following day so that the dog could be collected and begin her new life.

The next day was truly heart-breaking. A dog might only be an animal to some people, but she was my dog and I had raised her from a puppy. I hated the fact that I had to give her away to someone else.

Selina's mother's friend, Jackie, was waiting with me at the kennels while the kennel worker went to fetch Tara. I hadn't seen her in 4 days but as soon as she saw me she came running over, jumping up on me and trying to lick me in that unconditional loving manner dogs possess. It was a horrible feeling to just pass her over to a stranger like that. She wouldn't have understood what was going on either, and I felt like I'd let her down. She had been a loyal and faithful dog, yet here I was giving her away. It wasn't a decision I had taken lightly.

The next day it was time for Selina and the babies to come home from hospital. It's funny, we'd been preparing for this day for so long, yet now that they were here we didn't know what to do with them. There was no "good parent" guide for you to follow, it's just one steep learning curve. All they did was eat, sleep, shit, then repeated the cycle over and over. Night time feeds were also very taxing as there were two of them so we couldn't take it in turns. Every 2 hours we both got up to feed them, it was exhausting.

A week later we had an appointment to see the heart specialist about Fabio. After a comprehensive examination, it turned out to be a murmur. It would need to be monitored over the next couple of years, but with any luck he'd grow out of it once he was a bit older and more developed.

Technically, I was still self-employed but the income just wasn't enough. Even with my Army pension we were really struggling. I didn't want this, I wanted better for my kids because they deserved it. I would have to start looking for another job to give them the life they were entitled to.

Chapter 11

The Solitary Mind

I started to look for jobs right away. It had to be something with good hours and guaranteed work. Being ex-military I thought that a role as a security officer might suit me, as every ex-serviceman I knew seemed to be working in that field. I knew the wage wasn't going to be great but I also knew that I'd probably get the opportunity to do extra hours, which would help make up the difference.

I didn't have any savings so I couldn't afford to pay for the course to get my SIA licence. The licence was compulsory and I'd have to apply to the Security Industry Authority if I wanted to work in that type of business. It was by chance that the Job Centre was offering to fund a course for people who were registered as unemployed, to enable them to get back into paid work. I went along to one of their job clubs and was delighted when they told me they would fund the training costs for my SIA licence.

The next course wasn't due to start for another month, but when it finally began, I found that it was much easier than I'd anticipated. It was only a week long with two written tests and a physical intervention test to finish. I'd have to be as thick as shit to fail.

All that followed was a simple CRB check and 4 weeks later my brand new SIA licence arrived in the post.

I looked for work and didn't care too much about the location, hours or pay. At that point any job would do. A position became available working as a Port Security Officer at Cardiff docks. I applied straight away and was asked to attend an interview at the company's office in Bridgend.

Given the fact that I was polite, well turned out and held an exemplary military record, I was offered the job there and then. The pay was only minimum wage but they were offering over 60 hours a week, so I could live with that. When I turned up on my first day, the team supervisor issued me with a uniform before giving me a tour of the docks and the facilities. I was then led to the cabin that I'd be working in.

The cabin was very small, measuring around 12ft by 4ft, and the inside was sparse. There were a couple of amenities like a kettle, microwave, toilet, radio, plus a computer screen linked to the Automatic Number Plate Recognition ("ANPR") system, and that was it. I then learned that I'd be working here on my own. Alone in this minuscule cabin for 60 hours a week!

Two hours into my debut shift, the senior port security officer came in to meet me. He was a short, friendly chap in his early 50's and had previously held a senior rank in the Royal Marines with over 20 years' service. He knew that I had been injured by a bomb blast and that I had a few stress related issues, but he didn't know quite how badly these problems affected me. He presumed I might struggle with the job and although I assured him that I'd be fine, he told me that if I had any issues, not to hesitate, I was to go and see him. Maybe he could read my mind.

The first month passed by without any teething problems, and I was settling in nicely, content to be learning on the job.

However, I soon began to feel restless and would spend ages clock watching. It was a long day sitting in that tiny box alone. The job itself was easy enough, just lifting and closing a barrier, even a child could do it, but over the next few weeks my mental state started to decline. I was listening to the radio one day when it was mentioned that during a person's lifetime, their ears and nose never stop growing.

Well, I didn't believe this so I googled it. I wish I hadn't. The results took me to a disorder called rhinophyma, a horrible condition that usually affects those who suffer with rosacea. It affects the nose and causes it to grow bulbous, red, and lumpy.

I couldn't get the image out of my head and what was worse, I began to think I was developing the condition.

I was driving myself crazy thinking about it. Every time I looked in the mirror I could see my nose riddled with this ailment. What the hell was happening to me? I had no idea. I think the isolation did funny things to me - I literally had cabin fever. Over the years, scientists have carried out research on monkeys kept in solitary confinement, and it's no surprise that the consequences are never good. Even though my security cabin had two windows, I was still suffering from extreme anxiety and PTSD, in combination with the hyper active lifestyle I was leading. The effect on my mind was similar to that of a prisoner in solitary confinement.

As well as worrying about the rhinophyma, I was convinced my hair was falling out and this added to my already sky-high anxiety. Many nights at home I'd find myself crying alone from what this job was doing to me. I hated it, but with bills coming through I had no choice but to keep putting myself through the mill. I couldn't talk to anyone about how I felt, not even my wife. No one would understand how the job was affecting me so much. I no longer had a social life, the hours I worked meant I only got the chance to see my children on weekends as they were fast asleep in bed by the time I came home at night.

Something had to give and luckily, it did. An advert came on the radio for the Cardiff Half Marathon. In a snap decision I thought, "sod it, I'm doing this." I was no longer as fit as I once was, but that didn't stop me. I got my mobile phone out and signed up straight away. I thought I would make it a bit more interesting and speed march the course whilst carrying a 40lb military rucksack, and raise money for Help4Heroes. I announced my challenge on Facebook and set up a donation page. No more than 10 minutes later I received a comment from John, my former platoon sergeant during my time in recruit training. He was still serving, now a colour sergeant and qualified fitness instructor.

He asked for my phone number and said he would like to take part as well. He called me a few minutes later to go through some training plans, and we arranged to meet up in a few weeks for a training session in the Brecon Beacons.

With this future challenge ahead of me, I gained a new sense of purpose. It was something to take my mind off the mental torture of the security cabin. I managed to get hold of a military rucksack from a friend and started training at once. I even forked out £150 for a new pair of Lowa combat boots. They were pricey, but over time they had proved themselves to be one of the best boots on the market.

So, every morning at 02:30 I bounded out of bed, gulped down a quick cup of coffee, and was out the door by 03:00 with my rucksack strapped firmly to my back. There was an 8-mile route around the town and I completed it in 2 hours. Once I got home I had enough time for a hurried shower before leaving for my 12-hour shift at work. It was bloody exhausting but it was the only way I could train, work, and still have time to see Selina in the evenings.

While I was at work I was still suffering with my mental health issues, so I kept trying to focus on the half marathon to keep my mind busy. I needed to flood my mind with positivity to keep the negative thoughts at bay. Early one Saturday morning I arranged to meet John at the Storey Arms in Brecon. The Storey Arms is a former mountain rescue station turned outdoor activity centre, around 8 miles north of Merthyr Tydfil on the A470. With a large car park opposite, it serves as the main starting point for those attempting to climb the highest mountain in the Brecon Beacons, Pen Y Fan.

I was feeling reasonably fit as I loaded up my 60lb rucksack in preparation for our ascent. John turned up with a little day sack and I found myself wondering where his real rucksack was. Less than 10 minutes into the first climb, I was massively regretting taking my huge pack. I was knackered and couldn't catch my breath yet John was having no issue with his petite little day sack, trotting past while smiling at me. The 60lb had felt alright in the car park, but it was a different story once we were on the hills.

We ended up covering around 10 miles, a bit of a lung buster but a good day out. The next time we would see each other would be in Cardiff on the day of the race.

Every day I carried on training alone and made good use of the Brecon and Monmouthshire canal which was only a 10-minute drive from my house. In work I had a big collection bucket and couldn't believe the amount that had being raised so far.

With this new found energy, 8 weeks flew by and before I knew it, race day had arrived. My cousin had also served in the military and was doing the run using a rucksack as well, albeit it with less weight at 40lb.

It had been years since I had done a speed march of this distance, but I couldn't wait to start.

It was hard work but I finished in a fraction over 3 hours. I wasn't sure what time John had finished, but he was half way back to Bridgend by the time I crossed the line.

It wasn't about competing with John, nor was it about the overall time I finished in, it was all about the challenge and completing it while fundraising for charity at the same time. The day after the half marathon, I went into work with blistered feet, and handed in my notice. Without a doubt, working alone in that cabin had a damaging effect on me. I snapped my SIA licence in half and vowed never to return to that kind of job again.

Chapter 12

Endurance

With the Cardiff Half Marathon finished, I felt a great sense of personal achievement, and when I counted up the money I had raised it felt all the more worthwhile. The donations came to around £1300 which was a decent amount of money for a 13 mile run and would be put to good use by Help4Heroes.

A few weeks later I received the divorce notification from Maria. I always told myself I would never put myself through another marriage after the stress of the last one. With Selina though, things felt different. We had already been together for 5 years by this point, and with 2 young children it felt almost inevitable. A few months of saving for a ring and it was time to propose. Her answer was yes! We started planning the wedding practically straight away. Almost all the venues we visited were out of our price range which was disheartening, however, Selina's family saved the day when they told us they'd booked the Celtic Manor Resort for our big day. We couldn't believe it, the Celtic Manor is incredible and there was no way myself or Selina could have saved up for that venue ourselves.

My father offered to pay for the honeymoon, an all-inclusive Egyptian resort for a week. The wedding was beginning to take shape, the only downside being that I had to wear a suit. After wearing my smart military parade uniform the first time around, I now felt somewhat underdressed.

With everything in its place we had a stag do and hen party to enjoy. I ventured into Caerleon along with my father and uncle, while Selina and the girls headed to Swansea.

The big day was amazing, Selina looked beautiful in her dress. The weather couldn't have been any better, and the Celtic Manor was worth every penny. We ate some outstanding food in the Terry M restaurant, and then some more delicious food at the evening party, it was definitely a night to remember for a long time. We even ended up in the presidential suite, courtesy of the resort.

Two days after saying our vows, we travelled to Egypt. It was amazing, except for the first night when Selina's forehead ballooned to double the size after being attacked by some sort of bug. Thankfully the swelling diminished and we were free to make the most of our honeymoon.

Not long after getting home I began to look for another challenge I could do, one that was longer and tougher. I wanted to push myself to the limit.

After a few cold ones, a thought popped into my head from my military days. More specifically, from a time from when I intended to do the SAS selection course. Back then I was fit and determined but even then I knew that candidates were made to walk more than 40 miles carrying a heavy rucksack, and it seemed like a superhuman feat of endurance. It was something I wasn't entirely sure I was physically capable of doing. Even though I was pretty fit now, mentally I wasn't as strong as I was back then. Added to that, I would be training with an impaired knee. In the face of this, I was determined to attempt a long distance solo walk.

I was considering what suitable walks I could do when my buddy Mark, who I grew up with, suggested the Taff Trail. I'd never heard of it but a quick google search quickly brought me up to speed. The Taff Trail is an extensive walking and cycling route which stretches for 55 miles between the market town of Brecon and Cardiff Bay. It was perfect.

It was a simple plan; I would walk the whole way while carrying a 40lb rucksack, aiming to finish in 18 hours. I wanted to find a worthy charity and came across Scotty's Little Soldiers. The charity was formed a few years earlier by a lady who had lost her husband, Scott, whilst he was serving in Afghanistan. The charity organised day trips and the like for children who have lost a parent serving in the Armed Forces. For me, this was certainly worthy of some support.

I picked a date, Friday 23rd August, and planned to start in Brecon at 03:00. I solidly hit the gym every day to build up my stamina, adding in weight training to gain strength which would assist with both the walking and carrying the weight. Despite all of the effort I was putting in, I was still unsure whether I was physically capable of walking such a distance with that amount of weight in the time limit I'd set myself. Even in the military 10 years before, the most I had covered was about 20 miles, and that was as part of a team. We had platoon sergeants and physical training instructors providing us with morale and motivation. I was hiking nearly triple the distance and I'd have none of the support.

A couple of weeks before the event, a friend recommended that I cycle the route first to familiarise myself and get a feel for what I was up against. It made sense but I was concerned that it might turn out to be more arduous than I had imagined, and make me doubt my ability to succeed. I decided against it, reasoning that I was fit and determined, and no matter what obstacle I came up against I would just hit it hard and crack on, after all, as the song says, there 'aint no mountain high enough.

A week before the walk my uncle Dave said he wanted to take part. Instead of going along the entire Taff Trail, he would walk the 35-mile route from Brecon, to his home in Cwmbran using the canal route. We'd start at the same place, the Brecon Theatre, then walk together for 2 miles until we split to go ahead on our chosen paths.

The day of the walk arrived and sadly I had to go to work first, but the minute I got home I packed my rucksack with all my gear; plenty of food, first aid kit, head torch and batteries, map, spare socks and blister plasters, plus the crucial stuff like warm clothing, waterproofs, and a mobile phone. I also chucked in a pair of trainers, just in case.

For fluid I would carry 8 litres, 6 of which would be water and 2 litres of Lucozade divided between two CamelBak water bladders. I also carried a huge flag emblazoned with the charity's name strapped to my rucksack. I never did bother to weigh my pack but it felt heavier than 40lb, after all, I was carrying 18lb of fluid before counting any of the other kit.

As we intended to set off at 03:00 I would have to get up at 00:30. An early night was on the cards, not that I got one. I went to the local chippy at 19:00 to grab a pie and chips and was hoping to be asleep by 20:00. I was lying in bed when my wife put the TV on and switched over to the Big Brother launch event. Damn. I knew I'd have no chance now, I was tossing and turning and couldn't switch off I was so restless. I desperately needed some sleep but I was so psyched I couldn't relax. I went to sleep on the sofa as a last ditch attempt for some shut eye. It was pitch black downstairs and I even tried counting sheep but nothing worked. It was now 23:30, only 1 hour before I had to get up.

I did eventually drift off as I awoke to my alarm sounding, feeling infinitely worse for the small amount of sleep I'd managed to get. I would have fallen straight back to sleep had I not had this walk ahead of me. I sat on the sofa with a cup of strong coffee and a thousand-yard stare affixed to my face. I started wrapping zinc oxide tape to my feet, all the while thinking of the task that lay ahead. I was looking forward to it but didn't feel as confident now as I was so bloody tired. I'd only had around 45 minutes of sleep since 06:00 the previous morning, and the next kip I'd get would be when I finished the walk. If I finished, that is.

My father took Dave and me to Brecon and bang on 03:00 we set off from the theatre. For the first 2 miles we followed the canal together, with my flag catching on every low bridge I passed under. We soon got to the point where we'd agreed to split off and go our separate ways; Dave continuing to Cwmbran via Abergavenny, whilst I followed the trail to Cardiff Bay. I would be passing through a number of towns including Merthyr and Pontypridd, but first I had the mountains of the Brecon Beacons to negotiate.

The first 8 miles took me through some small villages before I ended up at Talybont Reservoir and the beginning of the Beacons. The next 5 miles were a real leg and lung buster as the trail climbed all the way up to its highest point, Torpantau. I was doing well for time, I had covered the first 13 miles in 4 hours and was doing well. It was pretty much all downhill from here, but still about 40 miles no less.

I trekked through Pontsticill Reservoir and the town of Merthyr, but by now my legs were aching and my feet were starting to hurt. I allowed myself a quick 5-minute break to carry out some running repairs. I had a few blisters beginning to form so I popped them and slapped some more tape over the top. Fresh socks now on, and the tougher terrain behind me, I decided to swap my heavy boots for my "go faster" trainers.

The next part of the course took me along a path that runs past the little village of Aberfan, the scene of the terrible landslide in the 1960's that sadly claimed over a hundred young children's lives when it destroyed their school. I could see the memorial garden as I passed by. With a bit of running, I soon made it to Pontypridd. I was feeling confident that I might just do this. I had about 20 miles to go, what's 20 miles? But I may have spoken too soon.

As I reached the roundabout by the university, the weather took a turn for the worse and my feet got soaked. Typically, I also managed to get lost. I carried on into a housing estate and lost the trail. I didn't have the foggiest idea where to go and there was no one to ask for help. I could have wept. Things had been going so well for me and it looked as though I may end up failing on the home straight. Thankfully my luck changed, and some local kids took pity on me as they spent 10 minutes guiding me back to the trail. It was a massive relief when I finally caught sight of the sign for the Taff Trail again, so much so that I got out a packet of sweets to celebrate. I was back on track.

I went past Castle Coch and was soon on the outskirts of Cardiff. This was it. I only had a few miles left, there was no way I could fail now. My father phoned me for an update and told me that Dave had done well but had ultimately jacked it in at Goytre Wharf, about 10 miles short. He had still managed 25 miles which was pretty good going considering he didn't train for it. I told my father I was near the castle roughly 2 miles away, and to give me half an hour and I'd be there.

As I neared the bay I could see my father waiting for me. I had tears in my eyes, some from the sense of pride in finishing it, but mostly because it was over. I'd gotten less than an hour's worth of kip in the last 40 hours and had walked over 50 miles alone carrying a weighted rucksack, all within 16 hours. I was physically exhausted, never in my life had I felt so fatigued. During the 20-minute drive back to Newport, my legs started to seize up and I could hardly walk.

As soon I got home I necked a bottle of Newcastle Brown Ale before jumping in the shower. Bloody hell, was I sore! My shoulders and back had been rubbed raw from the rucksack, I had nasty groin chafing and my feet were red and puckered with blisters. The second I got out of the shower I collapsed in a heap on the bed. Selina woke me up a couple of hours later when she got home, with a large chips and Doner kebab for me - what a wife! I needed to preserve my energy because the next day I was off on my neighbour Mark's stag do. Although I was massively proud of myself for walking such a distance, I swore afterwards that I'd never walk the Taff Trail again.

The next challenge I set myself was going to be on a treadmill. I was already a member of DW Fitness, so what better place to stage my challenge? I spoke to the manager about the possibility of doing a non-stop run/walk over 15 hours carrying a 30lb rucksack. She thought I was mad but agreed that I could do it there. I decided that I would raise funds for Help4Heroes again. A friend of mine from my military days, Lee Inker, asked if he could take part too. He wanted to raise funds for the Royal Gwent Hospital, Special Care Unit. I agreed to let him take part and we decided on Thursday 14th November as the date for our challenge.

While I was training, I planned to have another go at the Cardiff Half Marathon in October, a month before my treadmill endeavour. I was now much fitter than I was in my last challenge, so this would be interesting. The weight of my rucksack was going to be even heavier at 52lb. I parked at the Bluebirds Stadium, ready for the 2 mile walk just to get to the start line. It didn't matter though, as the rigorous training paid off and I crossed the finish line in 2 hours 12 minutes.

A respectable time for a normal runner, but as I was loaded with the equivalent of a small child on my back, my time was outstanding. I was almost one whole hour quicker than the previous year. I was now reaching peak performance.

Every day I trained hard at the gym, with long periods spent on the treadmill building up a solid endurance capacity. Three hour sessions became part of my normal routine, but even that didn't prepare me mentally for the full effects of lasting 15 hours. The day before the challenge my son developed a bad cough. There was no way I could carry out the challenge with the same symptoms he had, so I wore a 3M mask to avoid catching any germs from him. The morning of the challenge arrived and Lee and I were raring to go.

Most of my treadmill sessions had been between 2 and 3 hours long, but just a few hours into the challenge you could see that Lee was struggling. From then on, it only got worse. The gym became really quiet but the few that were there chatted to us every now and again. It was still going to be a long and boring day. It was 16:00 before it started to liven up a bit. Eight hours in and Lee had nothing left in the tank, his feet were sore and he was exhausted. Despite this, he had still covered 28 miles with very little training which is an amazing achievement. For the remainder of the challenge he supported me with motivation and cold drinks, while walking slowly on the machine beside me. I finally finished the walk at 22:00 having covered a shade over 52 miles, or the equivalent of two marathons. I wasn't as exhausted as the Taff Trail expedition but my feet were in bits.

Unlike outside where you get a mixture of terrain and the chance to vary your foot position, the treadmill belt continually wears into the same parts of your feet. When I got home I jumped into the shower and felt immense pain as the water trickled over all of the sores I'd developed. I had to recover quickly though, because on Monday I was starting my Gym Instructor Course in Cardiff.

I was really excited about starting the course. I was super fit and thanks to the endurance challenges I had already accomplished I felt like I was in a position where I could help motivate and inspire others to achieve the same standards.

Although I had declared to never take on the Taff Trail again, in February I planned to repeat the challenge. I guess you could put it down to the same feeling you get when you wake up with a hangover. Everyone claims that they'll never drink again, but that usually only lasts until the following weekend.

The charity I had chosen to support this time was for a young child from Newport called Casey Hard. The charity was called Casey's Cause and helped to pay for specialist equipment. Casey, a little boy aged 2 years old, suffered from severe epilepsy, cerebral palsy and spastic quadriplegia following a traumatic birth at the Royal Gwent Hospital. As if this wasn't bad enough for the family, Casey's father Anthony, a Corporal in the RAF, was recovering from brain cancer surgery. It seemed a natural fit to support them.

As the challenge approached, an old school friend of mine Jamie Boycott got in touch to tell me that he'd like to do the charity walk with me. I had no issue with this and after walking the trail solo the first time around, I knew it would be nice to have some company for the long slog ahead.

I went to visit Casey and his father at their home a month before the walk to collect some charity collection pots. I also contacted the local newspaper to drum up extra support for the challenge, as well as getting fancy t-shirts printed too.

As part of our training, Jamie and I went for a mountain trek over the Beacons. It was bitterly cold with a decent amount of snowfall as we made our way towards Pen Y Fan. All was fine on the way up, however coming back down was a scary experience as we got caught in a severe snowstorm just below Corn Du. Unable to keep our eyes open we had completely lost the footpath, "Neil mate, where's the path?" I heard Jamie call out. "Just keep heading down," I shouted back. Five minutes later the weather completely changed. The sky was clear and the sun was shining, it's amazing how the weather in the Beacons can change in minutes.

The day of our challenge arrived and without going into too much detail, it was a complete nightmare. First of all, while walking through the forest, we came up against a 12ft no access barrier blocking our path. Apparently there were tree cutting operations taking place, but we reasoned that at 02:00 we'd probably be safe, so we made our way through the barrier as the only other choice was an 8 mile round trip along the other side of the reservoir. Sod that. Later on we encountered numerous hindrances, like me dropping my brand new HTC mobile on the ground, smashing it to pieces.

To top it all off we ended up being locked inside Sophia Gardens, unable to go any further. We succeeded in covering around 55 miles, including the diversions, and raised a few hundred pounds to help support Casey.

Chapter 13

Out Of The Frying Pan & Into The Fire

I was still working alongside my father, trimming out the cars, but we were clashing all the time. We both had different ways of doing things, with different attitudes to life. Tensions were rising and I remember on one particular day, I'd had enough.

I slammed my tools down and stormed out. I couldn't take anymore. On the face of it it was a stupid idea as I needed all the money I could get, I was already behind with all of my utility bills. However, I felt certain that I would find another job within a week or so, I was a hard worker and had a good CV.

Selina wasn't pleased in the least but she understood, and said that no matter what happened, we would get through it together. I started by job hunt by sending my CV to every available job on Indeed.com. I must have sent at least 10 CV's a day but got no responses. I even tried phoning companies directly, but still no joy.

I was starting to worry now. The MOT on my car was due to expire and I was slowly getting unfriendly bills through the post. I was in a bad situation that would only get worse if I didn't do something, fast. I had no choice but to cancel all my direct debits as they were being paid out but kept getting returned, which in turn meant I was being hit with extra charges on my bank account. It was a vicious circle and I didn't know what to do.

My car was the first priority as I needed to get the kids to school, plus, when I did find a job I would need to be willing to travel. I booked the car in for a test and just hoped and prayed it would pass. I only had £150 to last me until I found a new job. The car didn't pass the MOT so on top of the £40 test fee, I was looking at a repair bill of at least £450. What the hell was I going to do?

I couldn't take out a loan as I had a pretty shitty credit score, and I wouldn't be granted an overdraft on my bank account either. Over the next few weeks even more bills came through. I kept quiet about them and didn't tell anyone. Realistically I should have phoned the companies to explain my situation, but I didn't have a clue what to tell them. I know they would have preferred some offer of payment rather than nothing, but I didn't have anything available to offer.

After a couple of weeks, a job eventually came my way, but like before it was a recruitment company and the job was working at a distribution centre in Magor. It was night work carrying out order picking, which didn't sound too bad. Because my car still wasn't fixed, I had no choice but to cycle there. It was only 10 miles each way but really it was the last thing I wanted to be doing with a night of work ahead of me. It was still work though, so I knew I had to give it a shot.

The pay was poor and based on a zero hours contract, meaning I was barely getting 18 hours a week which could drop without warning. My luck got even worse when, just a few weeks after starting and just before leaving for work, there was a knock on the front door. It was a chap from TV Licensing and Selina had only bloody gone and let him in. He told her the premises were unlicensed and that a report would be written up. She didn't know at the time, but I had cancelled the TV licence a few weeks before, along with the direct debits.

It might only have been £20 a month, but with no income it was costing me double that in bank charges. I explained to him why I had cancelled the payment and said I was going to set up a new payment plan online. Straight after he left I set up the plan online.

I was in a pretty shit situation. Although I was working, my income was still less than my outgoings and because I received a military pension, if I was unemployed then I wasn't entitled to job seekers allowance. I was using my pension to cover the rent.

Still, the bills flooded through the door. This time there were disconnection notices. I was really starting to worry now, and the pressure of the situation meant that Selina and I were arguing more. I could have resolved this by talking to my father, but I was angry and far too stubborn, so it was a relief when I finally got a bit of good news. During the 12 weeks I'd been on the job, I was nominated by the picking management as one of the most hard working and fastest pickers, and with a handful of others I was offered a 6 month fixed term contract. This was good as I was now guaranteed at least 30 hours a week. As great as this was, I couldn't shake the feeling that something was bound to go wrong. Only 3 days into my new contract I ended up housebound for a week on sick leave, with no pay, after bursting a blood vessel on my wrist. This was all I needed.

For the first time in my life I started to suffer from physical anxiety symptoms.

I was lying in bed one night and my face was on fire, you could've cooked bacon on it, it was that hot. I also started to suffer from facial tingling and brain zaps, the latter feeling like an electric bolt to the face. It was really quite scary. As well as this, I suffered with constant stomach problems and was always in some sort of pain.

Leaving for work one evening I'd gone about half a mile up the road when my phone rang. It was Selina telling me I needed to come back urgently. "What now?" I thought.

It was evident what the problem was as soon as I walked through the door. A bailiff was sitting on our sofa. He informed me that he had come for non-payment of council tax. I felt sick to the core and just wanted to cry. My wife and children were sat on the sofa as he began to do an inventory of our goods. He noted the TV and DVD player, our laptop, plus a shit load of other things. He said I could set up a payment plan to clear the arrears but would need to make a payment of £100 today. Bloody hell, I only had £110 in my account, but I knew I had little choice but to pay him.

Once he left, I felt like an outright failure. I was embarrassed and ashamed of myself. What man would put his wife and children in this situation? I hated myself for it which was made all the worse by the fact that I was trying my best to keep everything afloat.

While I was at work, my mind couldn't switch off from the worries at home and it was affecting my performance. I was still having the hot flushes and brain zaps, but a more troubling problem was my eyes. I began to experience blindness in work, I couldn't see anything. I was under so much emotional stress that my eyes had become extremely sore, constantly burning and watering. The only time I could rest them was on my break. I worked the night shift, so once everyone else went off to the canteen, I sat outside by myself in the dark. It was the only time my eyes could get any rest.

One evening Selina's nan invited us over and offered us £500. A gift to get the MOT passed on the car. I didn't know how to thank her grandparents for their generosity, and I was mortified about taking it. I would never ask anyone for help, I was too proud.

The next day I got into bed at 04:00, absolutely shattered. After a couple of hours sleep, someone was banging on my front door. I didn't go downstairs; I knew who it was. It was the bailiff. I wasn't in the financial position to fully stick to his payment plan and now he had come to take further action. He dropped a letter through the door telling me I had 7 days to pay £480 or he would return at 08:00 the following Monday with a locksmith to seize our things. Could it possibly get any worse?

The money that had been put aside for the MOT now had to be used for the bailiff, and to make matters worse, 2 days later I received a summons for the TV licence. There was a space on the back of the paperwork that I could use to appeal if I believed I had a good enough reason, so I began writing.

I explained that I was a former British soldier who'd been injured in a bomb blast. I let them know that I was receiving a war disability pension and due to unfortunate circumstances I was going through a period of stress and financial difficulty. I also made a point of saying that I planned to never let this happen again, and that since issuing the summons I had a purchased a valid TV licence. After a few weeks I received their verdict. Hello Mr Spencer, here is a £350 fine for you to pay, your payment card will follow shortly. I was extremely pissed off with this outcome. I felt they had no respect towards me, instead making me feel like a criminal. I was totally honest and up front with them about my situation, and demonstrated my willingness to comply by sorting out a licence that same day they visited me. I imagine they thought I was giving them a pack of lies, playing the wounded soldier story.

By this point I had almost had enough, how much more shit could possibly come my way? In spite of what was happening, I still tried to maintain a positive outlook on things. Family life was becoming difficult and my anxiety problems continued.

Selina and I were at the nursery waiting for the boys when suddenly the nursery teacher came running outside. "Can Fabio's mum and dad come with me quickly?" she screamed. I ran into the classroom to see my little boy lying on the floor, unresponsive and frothing at the mouth. It was too much for Selina and she burst into tears, running from the room. I wasn't in a much better state, lying there next to my little boy, tears running down my face and deeply concerned for his wellbeing. I felt sick and wondered if my son was going to die. He was having relentless seizures, one after another. His twin brother Nico was also in the classroom with the other children, but mercifully had been taken into the next room. This didn't stop him developing a stress rash all over his face and arms by way of empathising with Fabio's plight.

The ambulance arrived and during the trip to the Royal Gwent Hospital, he suffered from another 6 seizures. It was the worst period of my life. He was put straight onto a life support machine when we reached the hospital. He was only 2 years old, and to see my son having all these tubes and machines attached to him was breaking me. I was stressed to the max, and having to look after my son meant I wasn't making any money in work and would face even more pressure from the creditors.

For the next 4 days Fabio remained in hospital on the high dependency ward. Selina remained by his side while I looked after Nico back home. What Fabio had suffered from was called a febrile seizure, most likely caused by a high temperature. It was the most terrifying experience and one that I never, ever want to go through again.

Things continued to deteriorate. The stress I was under resulted in me and Selina separating. We were at each other's throats all the time and said nasty things to each other. Instead of working together as a team, we became worst enemies.
For me this was without a shadow of a doubt, the lowest point of my life, I honestly cannot put into words how this experience affected me.

The car now had an MOT, but only because I had used the money put aside for household bills. At that point, my car was the only thing I had.

Two weeks after Fabio's seizure, I was parked up in my car at the Hanbury Arms pub in Caerleon when I just broke down. My life was in a serious mess; my second marriage was over, I didn't know when I was going to see my children again, and I was homeless with only my car to sleep in. All of my personal belongings were in the boot. Worst of all was that I had nobody to turn to for help. In that moment I felt desperately unhappy.

I didn't know what the hell to do. I couldn't think properly; my head was spinning. I hadn't spoken to a single member of my family in over 9 months, but I knew I needed help.

I walked into Newport City Council Housing Office to register myself as homeless. I sat there, distraught. A member of staff asked me what happened and I broke down sobbing, I had lost everything and was now living in a car. How could my life have turned out so badly?

They couldn't help me, instead they handed me a telephone number for a military charity and told me that they hoped they could help. I suddenly felt both angry and sad. Part of the reason I was homeless was due to the stress caused by the bailiffs and their council tax, and yet here I am now, asking for help and they were turning their backs on me. I left the office fuming. "Sod your council tax", I thought.

All I wanted was my family back together, how could so much bad luck fall my way? After 2 nights in the car I took a drive up to the cemetery. I'm not religious, but I was genuinely on my knees at my mothers' grave, praying for a miracle to save my family. With very little money and no home, I had to do something, I couldn't live in my car forever. Even people I worked with could see that I was barely holding myself together. My work attitude suffered as a result, I was once one of the company's best order pickers, now I was one of their worst.

I contacted my father and also went to visit my nan. I never liked to ask for money, but if I was to get my family back, it was the only choice I had. I explained my situation and my nan agreed to help me. We ran through a list of the debts I had and she gave me over £2000 in cash, I couldn't thank her enough. Yes, it was humiliating and hurt my pride, but my family is what I needed and that was the most important thing to me. The money helped no end and I soon had all the bills back on track, and was living back home with my wife and children.

I was so happy to have sorted things out, but something had changed in me. During the struggles in the preceding 9 months, I felt like something inside me had died. A bit like when a boxer loses his hunger to fight, this was now happening to me. I had lost my fire.

When I got back to the gym, I couldn't find the motivation to train. I used to undertake 3-hour treadmill sessions and 1000 rep workouts with maximum dedication and effort. Now, after just 10 minutes on the treadmill I would hit the stop button. I was giving up on a regular basis and I couldn't figure out why.

Over the next few weeks, family life resumed its normality and all of my anxiety symptoms disappeared.

With everything that had happened I needed another challenge to build myself back up again, I didn't have the same enthusiasm as before but I needed something.

I came up with the idea that I could complete both the Taff Trail and the Special Forces Fan Dance route. To make it even harder I would do it completely alone, while carrying a 35lb rucksack and aimed to finish the 70-mile route within 24 hours. This was going to be my toughest challenge to date.

I settled on 9th January as the date and would raise money for 5 military charities; Talking2minds, Combat Stress, Scotty's Little Soldiers, Help4Heroes, and Soldiers Off the Streets.

With family life starting over, and a good Christmas now behind me, I felt revitalised and was keen to get started. The day I picked for the speed march couldn't have been any worse though. The UK was being battered by gale force winds with up to 18 hours of non-stop rain. However, I had now built a solid background of lifting myself up when the chips were down, and this was just another hurdle I had to get over.

Chapter 14

Blood, Sweat & Tears

The day of the challenge had arrived. I was nowhere near as fit as I'd been on previous walks, but I had the confidence to believe I could complete it.

At 06:30 I stood outside Brecon Theatre, contemplating the task that lay ahead. Despite the fact that the temperature was below zero, I hadn't bothered to put a jacket on. I'd done enough of these walks to know that within 10 minutes of setting off, my body would soon be nicely warmed up. Having a jacket would mean that not long after starting I'd have to stop to take it off, and that would be a waste of time. It might only take a minute, but with 70 miles to cover and only 24 hours in which to do so, every second counted.

I felt confident I wouldn't get lost. Having already walked the trail four times before and the Fan Dance a good number of times, I was well versed on the routes. I would go as fast as my legs carried me. As it was winter I was going to be limited to about 9 hours of daylight, with the rest of the time spent in almost pitch darkness.

I set off at a comfortable pace and after 2 hours I made it to Talybont reservoir, only to be met by a bit of a setback once I got there. The usual route I took through the woods was out of bounds, so I had to take the road on the other side of the reservoir. To be fair this route was easier and I started to wonder why I hadn't used it before. That was until I got to the last half mile. It was almost a vertical climb. I powered my legs upwards as strongly as I could so that by the time I reached the top, I thought I might suffer a sense of humour failure it was so difficult.

While I was making my way towards Torpantau, the weather hit. The wind was so bloody strong I could hardly walk properly. I couldn't help but wonder how much worse it was going to be on top of Pen Y Fan.

As I was making my way towards Cribyn along the Roman Road, the rain started to pick up. Thankfully I had gone out to buy some waterproof trousers at the last minute, nevertheless, if the rain persevered I'd look like a drowned rat by the time I finished. The weather was now making a Fan summit look unlikely. The wind was battering the hell out of me and visibility was down to only a few metres in any one direction.

I got to Jacob's Ladder, the base of the Fan, and saw a figure walking down the mountain towards me. It was a member of the Brecon mountain rescue team. He asked me what I was doing alone on the mountain so I explained that I was undertaking this epic 70-mile trek, and that I needed to climb the Fan to get to the Storey Arms before coming back over again. He thought I was crazy but agreed it was a hell of a challenge. Before he set off he warned that despite my best efforts and skills, climbing the Fan alone in this weather would be a genuine risk to my life.

After he set off, I thought for a couple of minutes about what he said. Yes, part of the challenge meant climbing the Fan, but in this weather was it really worth the risk? I didn't think so. I took the sensible option and opted not to climb.

Even though I now couldn't make the full 70 miles, I could at least have a good stab at my planned route whilst avoiding the summit. So that's what I did. Apart from the wind and rain that were still causing me problems, I was making good ground. It started to get dark again at around 16:00 and with almost 40 miles left to cover, most of it was going to be in the dark. The only real problem I encountered was while walking through a wooded area near Quakers Yard. The path was completely blocked by a shit load of fallen trees which I assumed must have happened that day from all the gale force winds. With a fence on one side and a 60ft drop on the other, my only option was to try and climb over the timber wreckage.

While picking my way through the mess, a branch caught my head-torch and pulled it clean off. It hit the floor and knocked itself off. Bloody hell, I cursed. I needed another torch to find the stupid thing, but I didn't have one with me. I began rummaging along the ground on my hands and knees trying to find it, and thank the Lord, I did.

The rest of the walk went by without any more drama, and I stopped for a quick selfie below Castle Coch. I looked terrible. I was soaking wet, cold, blistered, and high as a kite on painkillers. The photo was that good at capturing my plight that it ended up winning the Trail magazine "face of exhaustion" competition. My prize was 4 pairs of super high quality hiking socks.

After a couple more hours of pushing through the pain, I finally made it to the finish line. It was 04:20 and I had managed to cover a total of 64 miles in a little under 22 hours, bringing in over £1,400 for my chosen charities. The moment I got home, I wanted a nice hot shower. Standing under the water, I felt the pain hit me. I was aching and sore all over, but the buzz I got from finishing made the whole thing worthwhile.

Only a couple of months after the challenge, I was already considering another one. This one was going to be different though. Former Welsh rugby player turned adventurer, Richard Parks, undertook the challenge of walking up and down Pen Y Fan non-stop for 24 hours as part of his build up training for his epic 737 Challenge. I thought I could try the same thing but with a twist. First I planned to complete the Fan Dance, and then I would do the 24-hour climb. Of course, I would also be carrying a 35lb rucksack throughout.

An outdoor events company called The SF Experience ran a number of different events based on the UK Special Forces Selection Course. It gave civilians and military alike a chance to find out what recruits are required to do during a real course. It was ideal timing because in June they were holding the Fan Dance event. I thought this was perfect, I could do their event first and then go straight into my own 24-hour challenge.

Once again I started intense training, and this time I contacted the local newspaper to rouse some publicity for the challenge. A friend of mine from the military, Lee Umpleby, was keen to take on this special event which was great as more people meant more sponsorship. But which charities should we fundraise for? Talking2minds was one we both agreed on, but I also wanted to raise for another. I settled on The Cystic Fibrosis Trust as one of Selina's former school friends had a young daughter named Amy who suffered from Cystic Fibrosis. She was only 4 years old and also lived in Newport, so it felt right to be supporting a cause which would have an impact close to home.

With all the previous events behind me, I had good knowledge of what kit and preparation was required for such a feat, the only thing that could possibly let me down was my knee. It was still causing me problems, but I reassured myself that this would be the last challenge so I would push through if necessary. Funny that, I'd been saying the same thing since my first Taff Trail walk almost 2 years prior.

The night before the event I travelled up to Brecon. I wanted to make sure I had the best parking spot right in front of the Storey Arms. As the Fan Dance event was on, the car park would be pretty much full if I left in the morning, and knowing my luck I'd end up half a mile down the road. I needed to be as close to the Storey Arms as possible because my car was my admin point - full of extra food, water and other kit should I need it.

While to some degree it was good to get there early, on the other hand I was bloody knackered. I arrived around midnight and didn't get any more than 2 hours sleep. Trying to sleep on the backseat of my car was harder than I had anticipated. Not only was it uncomfortable, but every few minutes a car would come flying past at 70 mph, rocking my car in their wake. There were a few others in the car park who, like me, had travelled there early, but they were in transit vans and camper vans. They no doubt had a better night's sleep than I did.

At 06:30 I was already frying some bacon for breakfast when Lee turned up, closely followed by Jase and the rest of the SF Experience team. Even though I was tired I was looking forward to the day ahead. Unlike most people doing the Fan Dance, I wasn't going all out for time. I just needed to finish it before starting the second part of my challenge. The last thing I needed was to go all out on the Fan and then have nothing left in the tank.

Just after 09:00 myself and Lee, along with a few hundred other people, started the infamous 24km route. I felt good. I wasn't going too fast, I just kept to a comfortable pace while stopping to take a few pictures along the route. Once I hit the half way point at Torpantau, I stole a quick 5-minute break for a drink and some grub before beginning the return leg. I got back to the Storey Arms in a little over 5 hours and was feeling good. Lee had already finished and was chilling on the grass with a drink.

I grabbed a burger from the van and changed my socks ahead of our 24-hour climb. We didn't set off straight away but instead waited for the final runners to get home and the awards ceremony to finish. It had been over 90 minutes since I had come down from the mountain and my legs were beginning to tighten up.

We started to head up towards the Fan, but I couldn't keep up. My knee was fucked. With every step I was taking I could feel the cartilage crunching and grinding inside my joint. For fuck's sake, why now? I was determined to make it back up to the Fan, no matter what. It was a painful climb and seemed to take forever.

At the summit I had to make a decision. Do I continue and risk permanent knee damage, or call it quits and let my knee heal and live to fight another day? The sensible option would be the latter, but I didn't like to give up, in fact I hated it. I had put a lot of effort into training and raising funds for the charities so it was a decision I didn't take lightly. After talking it over with Lee, we agreed to call off the remainder of the climb. Our intention had been to summit Pen Y Fan up to nine times, and while it's possible, with a 35lb rucksack and a useless knee, it wasn't going to happen that day.

A few weeks after the challenge I was once again back on my arse after losing my job, and soon found myself struggling with only my service pension to live on. Fortunately, it wasn't long until I found a job working as a drayman for Carlsberg. I loved it and was getting some good hours in, it felt like life was heading in the right direction for once. I even joined a new gym although I still wasn't too sure of my knee. I had an X-ray and everything was as it should be so I was advised that I needed an MRI scan to check if there was any damage to the cartilage. My days of running over mountains with heavy packs was coming to an end.

Ever since I completed the treadmill challenge I had often thought about doing another similar venture. I really wanted to try and cover 100km in 16 hours, and last time I had fallen short. My new gym in Newport had recently been refurbished with some high end Technogym treadmills. This was promising, I liked it. I sent an email to the gym manager explaining my proposed challenge and the charities involved. I picked the same 5 military charities with the only substitute being Pilgrim Bandits instead of Help4Heroes. Two days later I had a reply...it was a GO.

Even though I wanted to cover 100km, I set myself a 16-hour deadline. Whichever one I reached first, that would be it. This time though, my rucksack would be heavier at 35lb. An increase of 5lb might seem insignificant, but when you multiply that by the time and distance, the extra fatigue becomes very apparent.

Despite the fact that my knee was damaged, it didn't give me any real problems on level ground. I was soon back on the treadmill carrying out some rucksack endurance training. It was nothing like before, just fast 5k and 10k runs. I had 3 weeks until challenge day and I'd decided to do it on a Monday as it was always busiest on Mondays and would help with the boredom. I booked the following day off work too, to give me sufficient time to recover.

While I was at work on the Thursday before the run, I suddenly felt ill. I could do without this now, I thought. I took Friday off work in the hope that it would pass and I would be well enough for the run. Did it get better? Like hell. It got worse. I developed a chest infection and laryngitis, and to make things worse I then lost my voice. I had no choice but to postpone the event.

I re-scheduled the event to be held in 2 weeks' time, again on a Monday and with plenty of time for me to recover. Steph the gym manager put together some new posters to advertise the run. I thought, if I'm ill again then I'm calling it off.

Thankfully, I recovered in full and was all set for the big day. The staff let me into the gym a bit earlier to set up. I had my mobile phone, headphones and charger, and by the side of the machine a large box full of supplies. I had 12 bottles of water, 2 cans of Monster Energy drinks, Mars bars, and loads of sweets. It was going to be one hell of a long day.

I had two vouchers that had been donated by the Army Parachute Association to support the event. Each one was worth £50 and could be used towards a solo or tandem skydive at Netheravon Camp. I told management that the first person to complete 2 hours on the treadmill next to me could have them. They said they would inform people of the incentive as they arrived at the club.

Instead of shorts I had decided to wear combat trousers because while they're only slightly warmer, they are a lot less likely to cause chafing which is never a good thing to experience on a long walk or run. The event was due to start at 06:15 and I had just enough time to go to the changing rooms and weigh myself. I would do the same thing once I finished, just to see if there was any difference.

I loaded up my rucksack and dialled 960 minutes - 16 hours - into the machine and hit the start button.

To cover the full 100km I needed to average around 6.2km per hour which doesn't sound like much, but with the weight I was carrying on my back and the humidity in the gym, it wasn't so easy. I kept to roughly 5.8km per hour, not too fast, not too slow, and kept my pace steady.

I passed the 50km point in just over eight and half hours, if I was going to make 100km then I had a lot of work to do. Physically I felt good, and I knew I was capable of running a bit if needed. It's a shame the same couldn't be said for my feet. They were in bits. Every so often my foot position would change and I'd end up walking on the blistered area. Before long that didn't matter though, as both feet were covered in blisters.

As the hours passed by, the pain in my feet really took effect. I was knocking back painkillers every 3 hours but they didn't seem to make any difference, and as a result my average speed dropped. I tried to work out how many kilometres I was likely to cover in my 16-hour limit, and it looked like I was only going to reach the 90km mark.

The last 2 hours became the longest 120 minutes of my life. Never had I walked for so long without stopping once. My body was in agony and I couldn't wait to finish. It was now 21:15, only 1 hour to go and I still had the skydiving vouchers on me. A young girl then got on the treadmill next to me so I told her that if she stayed on the machine for 45 minutes, I'd give her the £100 skydiving vouchers. She couldn't believe what I was offering and quietly admitted that she'd never spent longer than 20 minutes on a treadmill before. However, at 22:00 she walked away with the vouchers. Fifteen minutes after that, I finished the challenge.

Endurance. Picture taken near Talybont during the solo 105 Km speed March for 5 different military charities.

I didn't quite cover the 100km but still managed 88.2km, and boy, oh boy, did my body feel it. 88.2km without stopping, 16 hours of constant effort while carrying a small house on my back. I was totally exhausted, so much so that one of the personal trainers had to carry my rucksack and box to the car for me. I weighed myself after coming off the treadmill to find that I had lost 3lb in bodyweight, 4% body fat and burned 7,500 calories. Not such a bad day then.

Mental endurance. Sore and blistered after over 88km non stop on a treadmill carrying a 35lb rucksack. Undertaken at Bannatynes gym Newport to raise money for 5 charities.

It was undeniably the most mentally challenging event I've done to date, and also the most painful.

The result of walking such a distance left me with 19 blisters, two missing toe nails, and my back and shoulders were rubbed raw, even my backside was left bleeding. It was almost three weeks before my feet fully recovered. But you know what? I'd do it all over again.

Good times. With my wife Selina and my boys Fabio & Nico.

A Soldier's Story **The | Battle | Within**

Epilogue

To say that the 12 years following the bombing have been tough would be an understatement, although I totally believe it has shaped me into becoming a better person. From what I hear, the treatment and support for wounded soldiers these days has improved massively over the last number of years, and that is good news all round. However, I still believe that not enough is being done for those who bear the psychological scars often produced as a result of serving in the armed forces. It isn't right that soldiers are having to rely on civilian charities like Combat Stress, LINKS, and Talking2Minds to help rebuild their lives, no matter how much good work these charities carry out – it shouldn't be their burden to bear alone. It's time that the stigma of mental health was defeated and for it to be fully addressed and understood not just in the military world, but everywhere.

The wounded ex-service men and women who have suffered terrible injuries like amputations have to adjust to their new lives, and that can be tough and challenging, but I think in the long term they can sometimes deal with life's difficulties much better than some of those who are untouched. Why? I believe it's down to their wounds being visible. There is a lot more support available out there for ex-service members who have experienced physical injuries. Many of these wounded former soldiers end up with compensation and pension packages, as well as the entitlement to government disability and support benefits. Most importantly, they garner acknowledgement, respect, and understanding from the general public.

We need to remember that mental health issues like PTSD are also an injury caused by war. Yet sadly a lot of people don't see it that way. I think you literally need to be in the corner dribbling before anyone takes notice. THIS ATTITUDE MUST CHANGE! Unfortunately, it comes as no surprise to me that at least 7 ex-service people I know have taken their own lives in the past couple of years. Even more worrying is as far as I know, none of them had any bodily injury or were wounded in action. Such is the mental pressure these guys are under when they leave the services.

Lots of former service individuals struggling with their mental health can also find it difficult to get work or hold down jobs. This adds even greater stress to the person, causes financial pressure to their households and thus causes them even more problems. It becomes a vicious circle. Unless they are diagnosed with PTSD of course, but this is a challenge in itself! There just isn't enough support out there. So while we must respect those who display the physical wounds of war, let us not forget those with the hidden scars we cannot see.

How do I feel about the British Army these days? Well, I feel the same as I did before I enlisted. I knew the risks involved when I signed on the dotted line and I therefore agreed to play by big boy's rules. Yes, I felt a little let down by the lack of administration from my regiment, the Army Personnel Department and the SPVA following my return from Iraq, and subsequently the lack of physical and psychological support, but despite all of this, I truly believe there is no better career out there for a young man or woman than to serve in our outstanding armed forces. We are aware of the risks, so as long as you are willing to take a few on, the benefits of a military career are endless. I also believe it was the discipline and training I received as a young infantry recruit that gave me the strength to fight on through and beat these invisible demons, and to complete many of the tough endurance events I've accomplished throughout my life. Even though I have been out of the military for 10 years now and my career was cut short, I would do it all over again.

At the moment I'm waiting to see a knee specialist to find out what damage has been done to the cartilage in my joint, and am spending quality time with Selina and my boys. After 3 years of endless training and charity endurance events, plus the 2 years I've put into writing this book, it's the least I can do. Would I take on any more endurance events? For sure, if something worthwhile comes my way. As for the trauma and mental battles I've suffered throughout the last 12 years, well it's something I don't want to go through ever again.

THE BATTLE WITHIN

A Soldier's Story

Neil Spencer